RECREATION TRENDS

Toward the Year 2000

JOHN R. KELLY, *University of Illinois*

Sagamore
Publishing

a division of
Management Learning Laboratories

Champaign, Illinois 61820

Published by   **Sagamore Publishing**
a division of
Management Learning Laboratories, Ltd.
302 W. Hill St., P.O. Box 673
Champaign, Illinois 61820

Cover by   **Neil Dawson**

Printed by   **Braun-Brumfield,** Ann Arbor, Michigan

Copyright   © **Management Learning Laboratories, Ltd.**
1987

Sagamore Publishing
a division of
Management Learning Laboratories, Ltd.
302 W. Hill St., P.O. Box 673
Champaign, IL 61820

Library of Congress Card No. 87-71775
ISBN 0-915611-06-6

PREFACE

This book began with a practical request. A park and recreation district had to decide what to do with a school building they had acquired. Their fundamental question was simple: What kinds of activities would attract the most participants, not just next year but in the next ten years? What were the current trends in recreation participation?

There are a number of similar practical issues: public recreation providers have to decide on facilities and personnel; business entrepreneurs need to identify markets for products and programs before they make significant investments; resource managers must decide on the best mix of access, sites, and amenities. Answers to all these questions are based on recreation participation.

What are people doing as recreation? Do such factors as age, gender, income, and education identify those most likely to engage in particular activities? Is participation in an activity growing, shrinking, or remaining relatively stable, and most important for those deciding on investments, what are likely future trends?

There is, of course, no shortage of speculation about such questions. Often comparing data with quite different bases, promoters and journalists extoll new trends or even the latest "craze" without questioning the "common wisdom" based on repetition rather than critical analysis.

As will be explained in the first chapter of this book, looking ahead just isn't quite that easy. Data sources are inconsistent. Population changes may be conflicting rather than additive. Recreation trends are embedded in habits, lifestyles, resource opportunities, and economic and social contexts. Trends are not linear or mono-dimensional.

One surprise was that among all the data and publications there has been very little about trends. Further, the best sources of current information, the Simmons and Mediamark market surveys, were being ignored by most recreation analysts who narrowed their focus to the inconsistent and limited government surveys periodically conducted and made available in a variety of forms.

iv

This book does not incorporate every possible source of information or resolve all inconsistencies. It does bring together in an analytical framework participation trend data previously available only by expensive subscription. Also, it provides a picture of national trends. Such an analysis can be valuable background for specific decisions. It is, of course, no substitute for analysis of the particular district or market area for a program or facility. Nor does it replace a sound understanding of the meanings and contexts of recreation engagement. There has been a tremendous growth in research-based knowledge even in the last ten years that expands and corrects much that had been taken for granted in the 1960s and 1970s.

Nevertheless, this book is unique. It brings together previously unavailable information and analysis in a compact form. It may be read for its overall analysis of recreation trends. It may be used as a reference when particular activities are of interest. It may be employed by students and scholars as the springboard for critical discussion. For recreation planners and entrepreneurs, it offers a context for the analysis of specific communities and markets. It is then, intended to be practical, a book to be passed around the office and committee rather than decorate the bookshelf.

I am grateful to the publishing company for encouraging and expediting this book. Joe Bannon kept insisting that it was needed in the field. In the office, Lori Dawson did a creative job with the figures and layout designs and Nina Parsons did the input and formatted the unusual manuscript for printing. As always, I continue learning from my near and distant colleagues in the study of leisure and recreation and am grateful to them all.

John R. Kelly
University of Illinois

TABLE OF CONTENTS

Chapter 4

Chapter 5

Chapter 6

TREND PROJECTION GRAPHS

TARGET MARKET CHARTS

LOOKING AHEAD

The one sure thing about the future is that it is uncertain. We can never know with certainty just what tomorrow will bring in any aspect of our lives. The paradox of planning is that we usually base our plans on continuity and recognize at the same time that change is inevitable and inexorable. Nothing will be quite the same next year, including ourselves. Yet we plan and invest on the assumption that the basic institutional contexts of life will remain much the same as they are today.

That paradox of looking ahead will shadow every dimension of our project. We will be taking the best information about both continuity and change that is currently available. We will examine the sources critically and compare their implications. We will formulate projections about recreation participation based on the analysis of long- and short-term trends as well as on change in the population. We will put all this in an overall context of models and meanings. And then, when all this is completed, we will be reminded that some of the assumed continuities are problematic and some of the changes less than certain. Moreover, all the factors we will include in the analysis are interrelated so that a few small miscalculations could be compounded into sizable error. Let's look at two recent examples:

(1) It was fashionable in the 1950s and 60s to forecast a fast-approaching "leisure age" in which the former domination of productive work would give way to lifestyles with more free time and emphasis on nonwork activity. In fact, the future of leisure was defined as a problem by many who were sure that demand would overwhelm resources and that many workers would be unprepared to use this abundant time constructively. Projections even included exponentially increased needs for recreation professionals by 1980.

What happened? First, the projections were based on the long-term reduction in *average* weekly hours of employment since the 1880s. That trend continued through the immediate post-World War II years and then leveled at about 40 hours per week. Since 1960, economic cycles have led to unemployment rather than to a general reduction of the work week. Second, every level of the American economy including finance and production is now integrated into a global system in which advances in one nation are dependent on advances in others. Third, the projection presumed continued growth in the American economy, a projection rendered inaccurate by international competition and leveling rates of productivity. Fourth, the "average workweek" does not represent the wide variation found among those outside the factory, especially in the growing service sector of the economy. Fifth, other factors are involved in time use, such as the increased time devoted to work and maintenance travel in growing metropolitan complexes. All time not spent on the job is not devoted to leisure. Sixth, most of the gains in nonwork time were absorbed by at-home activity, especially television, rather than by organized recreation. And there were other factors. The point is that any simple extrapolation from one trend to complex social change is almost certain to be rendered invalid by factors that crisscross the field of social action.

(2) Today we are told over and over that we are far along in the transition from a "production economy" to an "information society." The personal computer on which I am writing is only one element of this allegedly profound change. Without undertaking an exhaustive analysis, we can sketch a number of reasons why this common wisdom is misleading. First, implementation of any technology has costs, not only in equipment but in personnel preparation. It is one thing to fold a useful technology into an economic system to increase efficiency. It is quite another to reformulate the nature of the system — how problems are defined and solutions are conceptualized. So far, the computer "revolution" is more a dramatic adaptation of new technology to old problems. As such, the revolution will depend

on the extent to which it is judged to be cost-efficient. In order to survive in a world economy, any corporation must produce and distribute goods and/or services in ways that compete effectively with other producers. Technologies, however dramatic, will be implemented successfully only when they yield a market advantage.

Second, the world economy still requires heavy industry, agriculture, housing and a variety of social services as well as electronic goods. Information is crucial, but "information about what?" For example, electronics has had enormous impacts on global financial transactions, but information is NOT investment capital. In fact, capital is required to support the information industry.

Third, the growth and recession of the electronic games industry illustrates that any technology, even in leisure, must tie into established investments, lifestyles, value systems, and skills. Electronic games will not replace the physical exertion, aesthetic involvement, or social interaction as significant elements of leisure styles. Technologies by themselves cannot completely transform complex cultures. The point is that electronic information processing is one significant factor in economic and social change, but it is not THE factor that will transform the productive needs of a world economy, the social patterns of reproduction and nurture, the personal values placed on community and biosocial self-development, or even reading. Already the costs of equipment, going on-line at a distance, and of the information itself, to say nothing of acquiring the skills of understanding and operation, have restricted financial network users to a small group that can profit from their scope and speed.

If we are now at least a little suspicious of those projections that base radical social transformations on a single factor, economic or technological, then are there viable alternatives?

Why Projections Are Useful

We cannot avoid trying to fathom the future because we plan and invest. If municipal managers are planning land use and recreation facility development in a growing area, how do they

4

choose among the alternatives? Once space is dedicated, personnel are hired, and buildings are equipped, it is costly to initiate activities other than those envisioned. Is racquetball going to replace tennis? Will aerobic dance fade as a fascinating fad of the 80s or will it retain a significant participant group? Will the time-intensive nature of golf limit its appeal? Will more and more exercise activity retreat to the home and to flexible times rather than be with scheduled groups? Will new neighborhoods have lots of children requiring playgrounds or post-parental adults seeking walking paths?

Answers to such questions require developing two projections: (1) Who will be living in the area? That is, what are the demographic projections? (2) What will their recreation participation patterns and priorities be? To avoid being trapped by a concrete set of provisions later found to be unsuited to potential users, recreation planning calls for looking ahead as clearly and completely as possible.

In both the business and public sectors of the society, the matter of investment must also be considered. Financial investment for space and equipment, personnel investment for hiring and training, and organizational investment for the development of program and products all require decisions based on projections of future return. Bringing a new product on line, for example, involves conceptualization, design, modeling, testing, evaluation, product design and tooling, marketing, distribution, and the assignment of all the factors of production to the complex process. If the potential market is based on some sort of recreation participation, then a projection of latent demand, alternatives, direct and indirect competition, and the basis of trends is absolutely necessary to minimize loss.

Why Projections Are Dangerous

If we had absolutely reliable and comparable data on participation trends and the precise composition of user groups, such projections would be relatively simple and trustworthy. At least that would be the case if all trends were linear — simply extending current rates of growth or decline. Reality, however, is that neither the data nor the linear assumptions are accurate. As we will demonstrate, analysis of most activities requires different data sets, indicating long- and short-term trends that are not directly comparable. We will have to "weigh" indicators, not just extend them.

Just as importantly, remember that trends are never linear. Business literature works with the concept of the "product life cycle." Every product, it is claimed, has a period of introduction. Unless it fails immediately, introduction is followed by growth in markets, a peak, a decline, and then a longer-term trend or plateau (Kelly, 1985). The same kind of curve can be identified in most recreation activities: an "activity life cycle" includes an introduction, growth, peak, and decline to some more or less stable plateau.

The issue is to identify in advance the likely shape of that curve. Will an activity or product be a fad with rapid growth and just as rapid disappearance? Or will it develop a stable or even growing participation base? We can be sure that no straight-line projection will be right. No activity just goes on growing, and any market can be saturated. But predictions are not impossible. The electronic game bust, for example, was quite predictable: consider who the participants were, how their resources were limited, and what social and motivational factors were significant.

How can we distinguish fads from trends, boom-and-bust markets from long-term development or stability? The numbers alone just won't do it. For any new activity — whether it is a sport such as racquetball or an activity such as low-impact aerobics — a number of questions must be answered:

- Who are the participants?

- How are their resources allocated in time as well as money?

- What are the requirements of participation in learning, skill, aptitudes, companions, access to facilities, time, location, and resources?

- How do those motivations and requirements fit into established lifestyle patterns and resource allocation for the participants?

- What resources are required for alternative activities and uses of time?

Analysis of the major market segment for video arcades, for example, showed a concentration of pre-teen and teen males, a very limited and volatile market. Further, the weapons-aiming electronics technology on which the games were based was limited in the kinds of skills required in the game formats. Even more important, the number of regular game players among other market segments, especially adults, was quite limited. A marked peak and decline was predicted based on identified limitations of the activity and the demonstrated participation segments.

In short, the composition of participants, the activity, resource costs and requirements, and the social contexts all must be analyzed to begin to develop reliable projections. That is the sort of approach that will be employed in this book.

Principles of Analysis

The projections offered here are based on several premises. None are esoteric, but all involve more than just extending trend lines.

First, recreation activities are not an independent sector of life. Rather, leisure, which incorporates organized recreation, is connected with all other dimensions of life. The life domains of family, work, and community all have elements of leisure woven through their hours and days, off-task activities engaged in primarily for the experience. Leisure is a context for the development and expression of intimate relationships, especially those of family. All sorts of off-task episodes and interactions color life in the office, store, or plant. Expressive actions are combined with developmental aims in church, child- and youth-serving organizations, playground, and school. The entire institutional fabric of the community and society are related to recreation choices, resources, and meanings.

Second, recreation choices and activities are limited by the institutional arrangements of the society. Schedules of time available for nonwork activity are shaped by work requirements. Economic resources depend on the reward system of the economy and our place in that system. Public resources for recreation are based on political priorities as well as the state of the economy. The kinds of activity that are encouraged or restricted are based on the value systems that are reinforced by religious and secular institutions. The contexts of recreation are opened and closed by the social, economic, and political system.

Third, hopes, aims, desires, and values are learned in that system. Further, they vary with our cultural background and the particular institutional contexts of nurture and associations. The roles that we take as students, workers, family members, and so on change through the course of life. What others expect of us and what we expect of ourselves, as well as the available opportunities and resources, all change as we move from childhood through youth and adult roles to the final periods of life. Students are not just younger than retirees; they are in an entirely different set of circumstances.

Fourth, recreation is a significant part of general lifestyles. Those lifestyles differ according to ethnic and educational background, by region of the country, and by age-indexed period of the life course. Leisure is central to the lifestyle of teens, integrated wtih nurture for young parents, tied to resources and self-definitions for pre-retirement adults, and sometimes more central again for retirees. Leisure tends to be integrated into overall lifestyle rather than separate from it.

Fifth, leisure styles, as one dimension of lifestyles, also show both variety and coherence. Most adults have a "core" of leisure engagement in immediate and accessible activities such as television, reading, informal interaction with important others who are available in the household or other regular contexts, and other at-home activity. Beyond this core, most seek a "balance" of activity appropriate to the life period: activities that are engaged or relaxed, strenuous or restful, social or solitary, demanding or disengaged, exploratory or familiar in contexts that offer a variety of social and environmental elements. That balance tends to change through the life course as the core remains relatively stable.

8

Sixth, the availability of resources is an important factor in participation. A family moving from Florida to Minnesota may switch from water-skiing to snow skiing. Team sports that are fostered in school are often abandoned as soon as school is left behind. Damming a stream and creating a lake will draw nearby residents into new forms of water activities. Provisions create demand as new activities draw participation.

These six principles suggest that recreation participation is shaped by a society's socio-economic context as well as by access to resources and opportunities. Further, both personal aims and social contexts change as we move through the life course. Insofar as recreation choices are nested in overall lifestyles, there is no definitive dimension of individual or social action that is irrelevant to those choices.

Sources of Trend Projections

These principles suggest that in looking ahead it is necessary to decide which factors are most influential and likely to shape both opportunities and choices. The contexts are as important as data on participation itself. At the very least we need to know something about shifts in resource provisions as well as significant economic and population trends. In Chapter 2, we will attempt to develop a framework for such analysis.

There are also complications, however, with our information sources on recreation participation itself:

(1)   There are long-term figures that concentrate on expenditures rather than on participation. Even when those figures are adjusted for inflation, the categories are not based on participation in any specific activities, nor are the data strictly comparable from one decade to another. As a consequence, only the most general conclusions about types of recreation-related purchases can be drawn. Further, research has indicated that there is no reliable correlation between expenditures on equipment and actual participation (Kelly, 1973).

(2) Despite an irregular series of national surveys on outdoor recreation participation, they are not comparable. Original data

have been lost. Samples vary from one study to another as do the activities studied, measures of frequency, and demographic measures. Recent attempts to gain consistency are too short-term and limited in their scope of activities.

(3) Other surveys such as the A. C. Nielsen series on sports and recreation are limited to clearly-identified activities with marketing relevance. The consistency of that series with a national sample was vitiated by its irregularity and eventual cancellation after 1982.

(4) The best current source of data comes from two national marketing surveys that are completed each year for over 15,000 households. They provide useful participation data from 1976 through 1985. The samples and measures of participation are consistent. New activities such as health club participation are added as they become recognized as significant. From these market studies, we can assess current trends for the activities they include.

Because of the limitations in data sources, the analysis must be divided between long- and short-term trends. For the long-term, only the most dramatic shifts can be identified with any confidence. In the short term of the last decade, however, the statistical basis for trend analysis is very precise for over 30 recreation activities.

Looking ahead, on the other hand, involves extrapolation of trends from the long- and short-term data, placing those trends in a context of relevant demographic and social shifts, and then weighing factors before doing any projections. The limitations, then, are only partly due to the data sources. There are also limitations of analytical perspectives. For example, since no one can forecast the state of the economy with any confidence, dramatic changes in the amounts and distribution of disposable income are problematic. Yet, with many kinds of cost-intensive recreation, especially where travel is involved, economic conditions are a major factor in future participation.

One other limitation should be recognized at the outset. We know that the rates of participation in almost any activity are different today for those aged 60 to 69 than for those in that age category twenty years ago. In the same way, those who will be 60 to 69 in twenty years and are now 40 to 49, can be expected to have different rates of physical, cultural, and travel-based recreation than those now aged 60 to 69. These differences are based on what is termed *cohort analysis,* which focuses on age groups born in the same years, moving through life experiencing the same historical events of the same ages, and entering each new life course period together. As with the military metaphor, they "march together as a cohort" through life. Cohort analysis presumes that each cohort reaching an age period will differ from those preceding in some ways and be similar in others.

Misleading Models

Quite a number of individuals and centers have established reputations as "futurists." They purport to tell us how the future will be different from the present, usually in a catchy and dramatic fashion. While some are far more sophisticated than others, many projections are misleading due to the adoption of unbalanced models.

The first misleading model is based on *technological determinism.* It is temptingly simple to latch onto a new technoloy and project a revised future based on its potential influence. The most recent such reductionist futurology in recreation began with interactive electronics, especially games. The premise was that because this technology existed and had certain capabilities, it would transform current behaviors and replace current forms of activity. Such projections ignored factors of cost, skill-acquisition, satisfaction, diversity of leisure motivations and meanings, social contexts, and as simple a factor as the marginal place of game-playing in most adult leisure styles.

The simple fact is that most technologies are never implemented to their fullest potential. They must be cost-effective, consistent with established skills and values, complementary to other dimensions of life, available, and satisfying in some way. Of course, if nuclear technologies had been fully implemented, we wouldn't be here to engage in anything!

Technology is one factor in social change. In some arenas, such as mass media and home entertainment, this half-century has seen radical technological change. Even in such areas as intimate sexual interaction, contraceptive technologies have had powerful impacts. These impacts were effective because they were consistent with established behavior patterns, value systems, and other technologies. The point is that new technologies are *adopted* — or not — because of many factors. Technologies may make social change possible, but they do not create inevitable outcomes.

The second misleading model involves gaining attention more than analytical error. The fact is that change is exciting, and continuity is dull. No futurologist will get headlines by proclaiming that the leisure patterns of child-rearing parents have changed very little in the last twenty years. To get attention, it is more provocative to announce that working mothers no longer have time to play with their children. True or not, such statements are picked up and repeated until they become the "common wisdom" of the news media. For example, "everybody knows" that the "fitness revolution" has transformed American lifestyles. The trouble is that most Americans don't exercise regularly and are measurably unfit, which has been the case ever since the Industrial Revolution and urbanization.

In our analysis, considerable emphasis will be placed on continuities. The best predictor of future behavior remains past behavior. Changes are more often gradual than abrupt, more likely to be subtle than dramatic.

Summary

The best summary, then, is simply that looking ahead is complicated. It requires identifying and evaluating a number of interrelated factors. This art, not a science, always deals in likelihoods rather than sureties, in relativities rather than absolutes. In the next chapter, we will examine some of the contextual factors that influence changes and continuities in recreation participation. Then we will take the best trend data available and develop estimates for the future.

In the meantime, there are two rules to keep in mind:

Rule 1: The continuity principle: The best predictor of future behavior is past behavior.
Rule 2: The change principle: Nothing stays the same.

References:

Kelly, John R. 1973. Three Measures of Leisure Activity: A Note on the Continued Incommensurability of Oranges, Apples, and Artichokes. *Journal of Leisure Research* 5:56-65.
Kelly, John R. 1985. *Recreation Business*. New York: MacMillan.

A FRAMEWORK FOR PROJECTIONS

CHAPTER 2

The contexts in which leisure styles are developed, resources are allocated to recreation, and in which decisions are made to participate are constantly changing. Every change, however, is not significant for the analysis of recreation patterns and trends. In this chapter, we will examine some demographic, economic, and social trends that are particularly pertinent to recreation resources and choices. We will also enlarge a bit on the cohort model in order to identify salient market segments for recreation. This chapter, then, is background for the examination of trends and projections of the resource, home, and community-based activities that will follow in Chapters 3 to 5.

DEMOGRAPHIC TRENDS: WHO WILL BE THERE?

Recreation participation in types of activities as well as frequency and style varies by age, gender, education level, ethnicity, and financial resources. Therefore, changes in the composition of a population will have impacts on recreation demand. Demographic trends for the 1980s and 1990s include shifts important to the identification of recreation markets.

(1) *The Greying of America*

The long-term trend is toward an older population. At the beginning of the century, less than 4 percent of the population was 65 or older. By 1980, there were over 11 percent in this "retirement period," with the percentage expected to exceed 20 percent by the year 2030. For most of the century, the increase came from the reduction in death rates in lower age categories. Now the age group with the greatest rate of increase is the "old old," those over age 75.

A second cause of the shift in age-group proportions has been the result of the long-term decline in fertility. Smaller families shift the percentages upward. Now the decline in middle-age and later-age mortality is increasing the absolute members of the over-65 age group. That increase is disproportionately composed of women over age 75.

(2) Fertility and Family Size

The long-term rate of fertility, that is, the number of children per adult woman, has declined for the entire century. Only a brief surge following World War II interrupted this decline. The rate was halved in the nineteenth century and halved again between 1900 and 1980 (Fuchs, 1983).

Several factors are intensifying that long-term trend. Delayed marriage for women, along with women's rising education levels, labor force participation, and early-marriage divorce rates have reduced the number of children desired. There are fewer husband-wife households, fewer women leaving the work force for childbearing and childrearing, and more women remaining unmarried (Masnick and Bane, 1980). The conditions for childbearing combine with the higher costs of childrearing to reduce the number of children desired. Every cohort except the "baby boom" crop from the 1950s is smaller than the one preceding.

(3) Household Composition

The makeup of households is also changing in consistent ways. Masnick and Bane (1980) have projected the trends from 1960 to 1990:

- Widow-headed households will increase from 9 to 11 percent.

- Female-headed households will increase from 17 percent to 37 percent; those headed by single women from 3 percent to 8 percent; and by the divorced or separated from 4.7 percent to 11 percent, half of whom will have children living at home.

- Households headed by married couples will decline from 75 percent to 55 percent.

In brief, about double the proportion of households will be headed by single adults. The increases will be most dramatic for women, especially the never-married, the formerly married with and without children, and older widows.

This means that in the coming decades, at least half of American children will have some period of childhood in single-parent families. They will have fewer brothers and sisters, usually one or none. The breaking and reconstituting of family units with periods of transition will be a common experience at all levels of society. Further, more and more adults will reach later periods of life without a marriage intact and with a history of family instability and marital dissolution.

(4) *Other Demographic Trends*

A number of other trends are expected to continue through the twentieth century:

- The overall size of the population of the United States will remain relatively stable. The periods of major growth due to immigration and fertility are over.

- Half or more of the growth will be due to immigration. Major sources of new citizens are Latin America and southern Asia. While language and other problems appear to slow the rates of assimilation, adoption of majority patterns through school and work force learning requirements are already under way, especially for the second and third generations.

- The geographical area of most rapid growth has been the South and Southwest, with 90 percent of the total growth occurring in the 1970s. A reduction of employment opportunity growth in those areas, along with factors such as water limitations in the Southwest, are already slowing this trend.

- The "baby boom" cohort now age 30 to 45 will continue to age as a population "bulge." In the 1990s their leading edge will enter the pre-retirement age period of those who have "launched" their children and who now have maximum discretionary income. They increase the number of persons in their ten-year cohort by over six million and account for over 40 percent more persons than does the preceding cohort.

- Education levels are higher for every succeeding population cohort. Of those entering the work force now, 70 percent have some college education, while the majority of those beginning work a half-century ago had nine years or less of schooling. Increasingly, some post-high school education is a threshold requirement for employment that is not marginal, unstable, or subject to replacement at minimum hourly wages.

Summary

The American population in the remainder of the century will consist of smaller families, more households headed by single adults, more unstable marriages, higher education levels, and greater population segments in retirement and "old old" periods of the life course. An anomaly is the "boomer" cohort born between the end of World War II and 1960 when the long-term fertility decline was re-established. The population of the United States is no longer increasing steadily with each infant and childhood cohort being larger than the one before. Even a temporary increase in childbearing by the "boomers" who delayed starting families will be dampened by marriage instability, women's participation in the labor force, and the desire for fewer children.

ECONOMIC TRENDS: INCOME AND EMPLOYMENT

A number of economic factors will have significant effects on recreation participation. While it is impossible to forecast the cycles and waves of economic expansion and recession, to specify the sectors of the economy most likely to prosper during any period, or to project income and inflation trends for the next decade, certain contextual elements seem well established.

First, the scope of economic enterprise and organization is now global rather than national. Finance, production, and distribution now involve world more than national markets. Corporations are international even when based in a particular economy. Therefore, the presumed relative strength of the American economy *separate from* world markets, production costs, and capital investments is no longer valid.

Second, the long-term trend for the American economy has witnessed a decline in productivity. Formerly dominant positions of major industries such as in automotives, steel, heavy construction equipment, and electric-power devices have been lost and are unlikely to be regained. The impacts for the magnitude and distribution of income in the United States have already been significant and promise to continue.

Third, labor-intensive production is being shifted to regions with relatively low wages. This shift, along with the loss of world markets, has moved more and more employment out of production and into the service sectors of the economy. Human services, health care, retailing, and other nonproduction employment account for all the growth in employment in the last decade. For overall economic health to continue and to support the consumer and service economies, markets for those goods produced by American firms and yielding a return on American investment must be maintained and expanded.

Through this period of change, the percentage of income spent on recreation has remained fairly consistent, an average of about 6.5 percent. That percentage is higher for those with greater discretionary income and lower for those with less. Therefore, the distribution and the total magnitude of income have impacts on recreation participation that are costly. Much of the expansion in recreation expenditures since 1950 has been correlated with a growing economy. If the world market and productivity factors suggest that the American economy is now in a low-growth period, then the demand for cost-intensive recreation will grow slowly as well. There are, however, two economic dimensions for which the trends are clearer than the global. They are the distribution of income and patterns of employment.

Income and Wealth: Who Has It?

American society is marked by great disparities in income and wealth. Entry-level and low-threshold service sector jobs pay minimum wage. Even for those with year-round employment, income before taxes will total only about $8,000 to $10,000. At the other end are positions in finance, medical specialties, and management with incomes of from $100,000 to $500,000 per year. A great many are running short of money for food and rent each month, while others are primarily concerned about investments that minimize taxation rates.

In 1981, 10 percent of households had incomes of over $50,000, a total of 24.4 percent of total earnings; 53.4 percent had incomes between $20,000 and $50,000, just over 61 percent of total earnings; 25.1 percent of households earned between $10,000 and $20,000, 12.5 percent of the total; 11.4 percent earned less than $10,000, less than 2 percent of total earnings. Figures on wealth rather than income show an even greater concentration in the highest 5 percent of the population.

The result is that the lowest end in earnings, up to 20 percent, has no "discretionary" income at all. At the other end, 10 percent have enough to be able to allocate significant amounts on leisure. In between are the 70 percent who are able to spend modest amounts directly on leisure, $500 to $3,000 per year, but for whom cost is always a major factor in participation.

There are no indications that the overall disparities are changing. Some analysts are suggesting that the shape of the income pyramid is being altered. The upper tier may be growing at the same time as marginal levels (Ehrenreich, 1986). In 1984, according to the Joint Economic Committee of Congress, the percentage of earnings of the top 40 percent of households rose to 67.3 percent while that of the middle 20 percent dropped to 17 percent. Unemployment and minimum wage jobs for the bottom 30 percent suggest that the marginal and sub-marginal household percentage may be increasing. If so, then recreation markets will be expanded at the upper end, but reduced for the lower 60 percent of the population.

Whatever the more specific shifts, the overall distribution remains one of great differences. Those differences will affect participation in all kinds of recreation that come at high cost, especially those requiring travel or access to expensive resources. Only an overall increase in real income, not likely in the global economy, or a dramatic shift in the pattern of distribution, not likely in the political climate, will alter the significance of income for recreation demand.

Employment Trends: Who Works and When?

The trend toward service-sector employment already introduced has occurred in a period of reduced markets for the products of heavy industry, general economic growth despite a series of cycles, and an increase in consumer markets based on rising incomes for major segments of the population. As a consequence, almost all new jobs have been in retailing and services with parallel reductions in some heavy industry and labor-intensive production. Some analyses suggest that the major exportable products of the American economy are now technical knowledge and investment capital, both of which are income-producing.

The service sector has been more likely than production to employ women in occupations such as retail clerks, nurses, teachers, and other kinds of direct person-to-person work. Further, those have generally been lower-paid occupations contributing to the fact that women have on average been paid only 60 percent as much as men for jobs requiring equal preparation. The growth in service employment has been one factor in the increase of women in the labor force, but not the only one.

First, the trend is long-term. Female employment increased from 15 percent for those aged 25 to 44 in 1890 to 60 percent in 1980 with a steady rate of increase at about 3 percent per decade to 1950 and 9 percent for the '50s, '60s, and '70s (Fuchs, 1983).

Second, the trend is related to other changes, such as the rising divorce rate and the need for more women to be self-supporting. Since 1950, however, the greatest increase has been among women with children living at home.

Third, the "women's movement" has stressed economic opportunities for women. However, the ideologies of the movement followed rather than led the changes. Greater attention to women's opportunities has been concurrent with increased requirements for women's income to support households and to shifts in the kinds of employment available.

Projections for households headed by two adults are that dual incomes will rise from 45 percent in 1980 to 65 percent in 1990 and to over 80 percent by the turn of the century. The trend is based on the patterns of women now in their 20s and 30s and the expectations of those now in school. The major change is the proportion of working mothers with children under 6, which is now up to 40 percent.

It is important to note that most employed women report that their motivation is primarily economic; they need the income for household support. This is especially the case for female-headed households. The trend toward employment is connected with the decreased likelihood of a single marriage that lasts until "death parts." Further, most female employment is at the lower ends of the income spectrum. There are a lot more female K-Mart clerks than rising executives.

Related to the trends toward service-sector and female employment is the dramatic increase in irregular and "off-time" work schedules. More and more jobs, especially those in retailing and human services, are in establishments that operate seven days a week and often 24 hours a day. This means that a high proportion of the work force does not work from 8 to 5 Monday through Friday. The consequence is that the demand for recreation opportunities may be less confined to traditional weekends, evenings, and vacations.

A second impact is the scarcity of time. All studies show that employed women with children living at home have the least discretionary time of any segment of the population. They must find their leisure in relatively compact and convenient periods and are least able to designate regular weekly periods for activity apart from employment, household maintenance, rest, and nurture and childcare.

On the other hand, despite the economic necessity of most women's employment, two-income families may have a higher level of discretionary income. Although much of that income may go into providing the time and household work substitutes that make employment possible, some may remain for recreation. For some two-income households, time is more scarce than income.

One other employment trend is just beginning to be recognized. It is that labor force rates for men aged 55 to 64 are declining. The rate, as high as 85 percent in 1965, has fallen to below 75 percent in 1980. Some of this reduction is the result of industrial layoffs in "sunset" industries. Some results from reductions of higher-salaried managers in businesses striving for more cost-efficiency. Whatever the factors, it appears that unemployment among the former "pre-retirement" age group, though sometimes masked as "early retirement," is becoming more common.

Summary

The two main trends in employment are the shift to service-sector employment and the increased participation of women. Both are based on fundamental economic trends related to the place of the American economy in world markets and economic organization of production. While the rates of change may decrease, the direction of the trends seems well established. The implications for recreation demand are based on income distribution as well as schedule constraints and household demands on women.

SOCIAL FACTORS IN RECREATION PROJECTIONS

Life is not made up of discrete factors, each of which makes an independent impact on individuals and groups. Rather, every change is nested in some others and has effects that are mediated through the culture and institutions of a social system. For example, as the cost of housing increases and residence sizes are reduced, the space available for both group interaction and for privacy in the prime leisure location, the home, is cut back. Some of this loss is mitigated by smaller family size, a concurrent trend. Nevertheless, economic factors of housing cost and income are interrelated with income, family size, and in-home technologies to change leisure styles.

Leisure styles are a part of "life styles." Those lifestyles are related to cultural and educational background, financial resources, climate and geography, occupational schedules and social expectations, type of community, value orientations, and social status. Within identified lifestyles, any change has impacts on everything else. What we choose is based on what we have learned, experienced, valued, considered appropriate and possible, and have found to be approved by others. Leisure styles are embedded in larger contexts, especially those of immediate communities of families and friends.

Nevertheless, there have been a number of attempts to characterize lifestyles that are useful in understanding social and economic interrelationships. Before identifying a number of continuities and changes in leisure styles, it would seem useful to introduce examples of more inclusive lifestyle typologies.

Some of the typologies are primarily psychological in their analysis. Most have some sort of progression from inadequacy to full functioning. Abraham Maslow's (1954) progression is based on the accomplishment of tasks along a continuum from fundamental survival and security through social belonging and esteem to self-actualizing and creative action. Leisure becomes particularly important as a context for the activity that goes beyond survival and seeking a place in society to self-creating activity. Erich Fromm (1955) combines developmental psychology and economic orientations in his typology of those who progress through stages of hoarding and exploitative marketing to truly productive lives in community with others. David Riesman (1950) produced a typology based on where people look for the values and images with which they identify. The "inner-directed" are contrasted with the "outer-directed," as well as with those oriented primarily to tradition or those who are fundamentally autonomous.

All of these typologies have implications for what individuals will seek in their recreation—their styles and motivations, as well as locales and kinds of activity. Few analysts, however, have focused on leisure and recreation in developing their typologies. Focus has tended to be on economic roles and interpersonal relationships. More recently, leisure has been included in lifestyle typologies:

(1) The simplest is based on a study of adults aged 40 and above in a Midwestern community (Kelly, 1987). The typology

is based on the concept of "life investment." The domains in which people invest their resources, find their identities, and from which they receive support characterize different orientations to life. The largest number of the adult sample was found to be "balanced investors" who directed their resources and commitments toward at least two of the three life domains of work, family, and leisure. For them, leisure was not a separate segment of life, but was integrated into a balanced set of investments that had considerable continuity through the life course. The second significant group was "family-focused." For them, both work and leisure tended to be instrumental, valued as they contributed to the development and expression of family relationships. The other two types of significance reflected a lack of access to satisfying relationships and opportunities. They were limited or deprived of opportunity through the life course. Somewhat surprisingly, primary focus on either leisure or work to the exclusion of other domains was extremely rare among those over-40 adults. One primary difference between the "balanced investors" and the "family-focused" was in leisure. The "balanced investors" were most likely to value their leisure investments as an integral and important domain of life rather than simply as a context for family interaction.

(2) The second recent typology that includes leisure as a basis of distinction is derived from the Values and Lifestyles Program (VALS) of the Stanford Research Institute International (Mitchell, 1983). This market segmentation typology is based on a national sample and brings together dimensions of work, family and intimacy, community, leisure, and value orientations, along with access to economic and social resources. The first division consists of those who are "need-driven" and struggle with scarcity. Those with greater resources are divided between the inner-directed and the outer-directed with the proposed possibilty of an integrated style. Factors in the categorization include period in the life course, educational background, economic position and resources, and psychological predispositions, as well as social and political values. A summary of the nine styles follows:

The Need-driven:

- Survivors who are older, poor, fearful, and preoccupied with getting through the day and week (4 percent).
- Sustainers on the edge of poverty who have strategies for making it despite being economically and socially marginal (7 percent).

The Inner-directed:

- "I-am-me" self-centered and self-preoccupied youth who exemplify the dilemma of wanting both individuality and acceptance from their peers. This transitional group is quite leisure-oriented on their way to more adult styles (5 percent).
- Experiential younger adults who are oriented toward personal growth and development and for whom leisure is central to their values (7 percent).

The Outer-directed:

- Belongers who are aging, traditional, conventional, and oriented toward family values. Such "middle-mass" Americans constitute 35 percent of the adult population.
- Emulators who are younger and ambitious and trying to achieve a place in the system. They use leisure for acceptance (9 percent).
- Achievers who believe they have made it in social and economic positions or who are well on the way. Leisure may be secondary to status roles (22 percent).

Finally, there is the possibility of an "integrated" lifestyle of relatively mature and autonomous adults who direct their lives according to flexible images, relate in accepting ways to others, and whose lives are integrated in development appropriate to the period in their life course. The integrated are estimated to be only about 2 percent of the adult population.

The VALS research group has employed this typology to distinguish market segments for a variety of goods and services. They believe that such a typology is more useful than the usual demographic profiles in identifying those who make certain market choices and why they make those choices. At least they offer an approach to understanding how age, economic standing, and social status are indices of lifestyles that combine several dimensions. Leisure choices and investments are one integrated dimension of these lifestyles, rather than a segmented and residual set of behaviors.

(3) Market segmentation, however, need not deny such inclusive lifestyle typologies to identify different leisure and recreation styles. Important differences are based on the more traditional factors of age, gender, family status, and economic resources. For example, recreation market segments can be distinguished by socio-economic categories such as the following:

Stable Market Segments:

- *High-end* consumers whose incomes and assets enable them to afford major expenditures for whatever leisure they value most. Their travel is expensive and extensive. They are the major market for high-cost items such as prestige resorts, exclusively-located second homes, and big-ticket deluxe travel.

- *Blue collar* workers now augmented by low-pay and low-skill clerical workers and retail employees. Their major expenditures on leisure, if any, are made before they are 50 years old. They seldom have a significant vested pension resource, are most likely to live in rental housing, and have limited health care. Their incomes are directed primarily toward "necessities" of maintenance. They are a sizable recreation market, but mostly for at-home and community programs and resources with low cost thresholds.

- The *poverty class* whose lack of economic security intensifies maintenance problems in health, housing, nutrition, and transportation. Their leisure tends to be close to home and relatively cost-free, such as television and informal interaction.

Changing Market Segments:

- The *new class* with university degrees and managerial or technical employment. They have adequate but not unlimited discretionary income and expect to spend a portion of it on leisure. They have had a range of recreation experiences and usually have plans for expansion in the future. Their residence-base activity is important to them, but they also expect to travel and be involved in sport, cultural, and other community-based engagements. They are urban or suburban in location, often depending on life course period and the age of children. Their tastes are cosmopolitan, but they take the nurture of one or two children very seriously. Almost all who are married are dual-income households.

- The *middle mass* have experienced relatively stable but limited work histories. More than their predecessors they may have two incomes, experience marital instability, and have small families. Investment in a residence is central. Their tastes are not sophisticated, but they believe they have the right to some enjoyable activity. They travel on a budget and usually by car. They are a major market segment for goods and services that support their lifestyles even though they tend to be very price-conscious. They may, however, invest in major items such as boats or vehicles that facilitate major interests.

Each of these five categories can be subdivided according to other salient factors. There are important gender differences in experiences, tastes, and expectations. Those in childbearing and childrearing periods of the life course tend to center much of their recreation around their children in all the five categories. Older persons with health problems have a constricted scale of recreation with smaller circles of social interaction and activities located in or closer to home. Those in the midst of family transition or disruption tend to orient more of their leisure toward finding new social contexts for activity and relationships.

Therefore, age, family status, and gender are all significant variables that affect recreation choices for each of the socio-economic groups and segment the recreation market. In the activity trend analysis in the next three chapters, we will refer to these segments and to the factors that cut across them to identify those market segments most likely to increase or decrease in participation.

Another important factor is that of education. For those above poverty levels and within age categories, there is nothing that indexes the likelihood of different kinds of recreation participation as clearly as the amount and quality of education. Education not only is an index of resources and opportunities, but also of the probability of experience with a variety of leisure activities and opportunities. Fortunately, the market studies on which we will base our current trend analyses include age, income, education level, and gender breakdowns.

LEISURE STYLES AND RESOURCES

Leisure Resources

For each market segment, chances in access to resources are already affecting leisure styles and choices. A summary of some of those changes includes time and space as well as financial, social, and skill resources:

Time: The general leveling of average employment hours is different for different occupations. Retail and service occupations have schedules that are more diverse and irregular. Time for recreation often does not occur on weekends and evenings. Also, time is becoming a resource more scarce for single parents, dual-income households, commuters in crowded metropolitan areas, and a resource salaried employees of businesses that attempt to increase productivity. The alleged "growth in free time' is uneven at best and inaccurate for most adults in the 1980s.

Space: Housing and energy costs are reducing the proportion of the population who will live in detached homes with considerable recreation space. Multiunit housing and space-efficient design will reduce the at-home leisure space. At the same time, metropolitan areas will continue to grow, even if at decreasing rates. The resulting high cost of indoor and outdoor space limits the expansion of public and business provisions for recreation. Activities that require costly space will be limited by the ability of tax-supported agencies and users to pay for it.

Money: The distribution of income already outlined may be changing somewhat. Reductions in the size of blue-collar and

28

white-collar clerical groups will decrease that segment of the recreation markets. The possible growth in "new class" size with their discretionary incomes might be balanced by the simultaneous growth of the segment whose incomes are close to marginal and whose employment is insecure. The stable if limited middle mass category—the consistent markets for many kinds of public recreation as well as goods and services—may be reduced in size. As a consequence, more marketing attention will be given to the "new class" with their greater resources and orientations that place major value on leisure.

Social resources: Smaller families, increased family dissolution, the separation of work and residential locales, geographical mobility increased by employment shifts, and increased at-home entertainment have all affected the development of skills for activities that require regular interaction with other people. It may be harder and harder to gather a group for such activities as team sports, classes in the arts, political action, or organization building.

Skills: Higher education levels will raise the depth and breadth of skill repertoires for a variety of recreation activities. More and more people have had opportunities to gain interests and experience with activities previously reserved for the affluent. This may be a snowballing trend as more such families introduce their children to leisure possibilities and skill-acquisition. Resources for such experiences may, however, be reduced for some who fall back from previous levels of economic stability.

In general and except for space, trends seem to be toward greater resources for recreation, but they are neither universal nor consistent. Households with more financial resources may have less time. Economic shifts in employment patterns and stability will affect more households throughout the life course. Therefore, market segmentation could focus increasingly on minorities with disproportionate resources of every kind.

Leisure Styles

A common formula in marketing is the "20-80 rule." The proposition is that in most markets 20 percent of the total make up

80 percent of the actual demand. Translated to recreation, the rule would suggest that the 20 percent of the most active participants in an activity do 80 percent of the total participation as measured by frequency and duration. It would also imply that the 20 percent who are most committed to an activity constitute 80 percent of the demand for resources, facilities, equipment, and instruction.

This focus on the minority who are most committed to particular recreation activities is reinforced by marketing research that has found that between 20 percent and 30 percent of those who engage in an activity at all do so with regularity. Leisure participation choices are not separate from the overall patterns of resource allocation of any lifestyle. Rather, we allocate our resources and respond to opportunities according to learned value systems. A current study based on the national survey of markets and media used by Mediamark Research, Inc., found that American adults are divided almost evenly between those engaged in a variety of leisure investments ("Actives") and those who are only peripherally involved in active engagements ("Passives"). The Actives are younger, with 45 percent aged 18 to 34 vs 21 percent of the Passives; another 21 percent of the Passives are aged 65 and over compared with 10 percent of the Actives. Actives are twice as likely to have attended college and live in households headed by those in professional or managerial occupations. A majority of those in the lowest income categories are Passives, while Actives are most often found in the highest categories. Middle income adults are about evenly divided. In short, Actives are those with the most resources: social, economic, and age-indexed physical capabilities. Note, however, the ratios are about 2:1. Actives may also be older, of moderate incomes, less educated and generally identifiable as members of the middle mass.

The Actives are further divided into seven leisure styles based on the mode and locales of their consistent activity engagements:

- "Outdoor energetics" are men and women, usually young, who engage regularly in resource-based activity such as skiing and sailing and community activity such as running and tennis.

- "On your toes" are young affluent females who are into dancing, health clubs, and aerobics.
- "Surf and turf" are the men who hunt and fish.
- "Cerebrals" are the game players — chess, backgammon, and others.
- "Home and hearth" concentrate on home entertaining and activities.
- "Gentle pursuits" include gardening, bird watching, etc.
- "Creatives" are engaged as performers and producers in the arts and in home-based crafts.

These types are derived from a cluster analysis of the Mediamark national survey of 20,000 households and are reported in a marketing study entitled *Leisurestyles* (1986). The technique is useful for identifying activities that distinguish participation groups. The study found that about half of all adults are "Actives" who make up a disproportionate share of markets for leisure goods and services. The half who are "Passives" tend to watch television, engage in informal activity around the home, and take fairly traditional vacation trips by car. They are in many cases the "Family-focused."

The Core plus Balance Model

The stylistic distinction that identifies market segments based on activity clusters is limited because it does not incorporate what most of them have in common. Reanalysis of a number of studies has revealed that most adults have a *core* of activities that remain central to their leisure patterns throughout the life course. This core includes watching television and reading, informal interaction with family and friends, walking, doing projects around the residence, and playing with children. These are low-cost and easy-access activities that do not require special plans, expenditures, resources, or skills. Beyond this core, most adults have a *balance* of activities that reflects developed interests and changes somewhat through the life course. Particular sports, outdoor activities, cultural engagement, travel environments, and skill-based activities reflect age, education level, community and regional resources, and family status. While some people concentrate on one kind of activity, more seek a balance of strenuous and relaxing, social and solitary, physical and intellectual, exploratory and familiar, and demanding and comfortable engagements. Although it is possible to identify leisure style differences, it is also important to note that the groups are not completely discrete. Overlaps and commonalities blur the differences.

COHORT ANALYSIS AND LIFESTYLES

A series of principles underlies the projections that will follow in Chapters 3 to 5:

First, continuities and consistent behaviors are just as important as change.

Second, recreation participation will be affected by major population and economic shifts that include fertility and family size, marriage and divorce patterns, aging longevity, service sector employment and schedules, women's employment, the distribution of income, and the overall strength of the economy.

Third, recreation choices and investments are made in the context of more general lifestyles that are related to age, family status, education level, and income.

Fourth, recreation preferences and engagements change through the life course in relation to resources, role expectations, and abilities. Nevertheless, a core of accessible activities persists through the life course for most adults.

Fifth, age itself may be misleading in future projections because those who are now in their 30s may have different patterns in twenty years from those now in their 50s. There are shifts in health, expectations, past experience, and resources. Therefore, "cohort analysis" will be the model employed. Cohort differences such as consistently rising education levels will shape likely leisure styles in the future. While involving multiple factors, estimates can be reasonably reliable for a period as short as a decade or even two.

Sixth, recreation activities are seldom fixed for any individual moving through the life course. There are almost always alternative activities and environments, sometimes in direct competition for time and other resources. Recreation demand, therefore, cannot be estimated in quite the same way as the future demand for refrigerators or frozen vegetables. Recreation choices are subject to influence by companions, weather, crowded facilities, conflicting timetables, and countless other factors. The value placed on a particular activity, therefore, is related to consistency of participation. We will use frequency figures, then, to distinguish those who are committed to any activity from those who are occasional participants.

Market Segmentation

It is, of course, impossible to include every possible factor in every analysis. Our aim is to identify general trends rather than to provide a complete analysis of participation in any one activity. Further, some kinds of information are consistent and available while others are incomparable and esoteric. Therefore, the identification of demand groups for particular activities will use available trend data as indices for more complex factors. Although their significance varies from activity to activity, age, gender, education level, income, and family status are the factors that have been found most consistently reliable in distinguishing regular participants from occasional and nonparticipants.

Further, these variables can help identify the cohorts that will be in the various age categories in 1990 and 2000. For example, the "baby boom" cohort has been identified as they moved out of school into early establishment periods and childrearing and in time entered postparental and retirement periods of the life course.

These variables will be used to identify the market segments most significant for each kind of activity. In many cases we can identify the following:

- *Growth markets* that promise increased participation
- *Established markets* that promise consistency of demand
- *Potential markets* that can be developed in the future
- *Low probability markets* that offer only slight chances for growth

The projections, then, will be based on past participation, consistencies as well as trend trajectories, and on identification of life style groupings based on economic and social factors.

CONTINUITIES AND CHANGES: A SUMMARY

Before going on to the projections for particular activities, one further review will offer a more complete background on leisure in general: the continuities and changes in leisure contexts, resources, styles, and meanings.

Continuities in Leisure and Recreation

(1) The 6.5 percent rule of leisure expenditures indicates that an infinite expansion of recreation spending cannot be anticipated. Even though the key concept is *discretionary* income—and those who have higher incomes tend to exceed the 6.5 percent average—expenditures have consistent limits, especially when the economy is not growing.

(2) The "core plus balance" model remains valid through the life course. Special recreation activities are part of more comprehensive leisure and lifetyles that include regular participation by most adults in accessible activity, especially at home.

(3) Leisure is embedded in the life course with its continuities and changes. As a consequence, both meanings and activities shift somewhat as individuals age, take up and drop various family and work roles, and change in interests and self-definitions.

(4) Time remains scarce for most adults. The time costs of recreation participation may be a greater constraint than financial costs, especially for dual-income households with children.

(5) The one really profound social revolution of our era is in the sexual realm. Major behavioral changes since the 1950s permeate every aspect of the society, including leisure. Sexual expression is accepted, diversity is legitimized, and sexuality is presumed as a dimension of activity. Recreation meanings and choices have recognized sexual dimensions even when focused on a specific activity or environment. Intimate relationships will continue in diverse contexts other than those of marriage and the family.

(6) Considerable recreation involves self-display and style. How participants manage impressions to gain approval and acceptance involves styles of participation, clothing, equipment,

and being with the "right" companions. Impression-management may be more important than the game for some leisure events.

(7) The distance costs of recreation continue to mount in growing urban areas. Distance is translated into time costs increased by crowding and "rush hour" timetables that affect leisure as well as work. Private transportation may be a recreation necessity for time-efficiency.

(8) Race-intensified poverty, especially in urban ghettoes and rural fringes, is set against the affluent life and leisure styles portrayed on television. Anger and alienation may focus on leisure as much as on economic rewards and opportunity.

(9) Shopping continues as a central leisure activity for American adults, both in the home community and while travelling. Shopping malls and boutique boulevards are major leisure environments.

(10) Travel remains important for adults even when styles and costs vary widely. In 1980, 130 million Americans took trips of ten days or longer, 85 percent by car. Styles, however, are very different for the rich in comparison to the middle mass or for parents in comparison to the retired.

(11) Leisure and recreation investments are an important component of marriage and family life. For both intact and serial marriages, recreation choices can be conflict-ridden at the same time that they are contexts for expressing and developing relationships. Disappointment in leisure companionship and support can be a major factor in marriage dissolution.

(12) Developmental aims for families with children will be important in selecting recreation investments. Parents, perhaps especially those with only one or two children, will seek recreation that will improve their children's chances to compete in the worlds of school and work.

(13) Every younger cohort has a higher level of education with consequent variety of leisure interests and experiences.

(14) The quality of relationships remains central to satisfaction with most recreation experiences.

(15) Concerns over the environment will continue to be balanced against development for recreation and other uses.

(16) The trend toward securing blocks of time — long weekends as well as vacations — for leisure engagements will also continue. Travel-based activity will remain special, but somewhat more frequent.

(17) The trend toward more independence and self-reliance for women will also continue. This means that women's interests will become more and more important in determining patterns and resource allocation.

Changes in Leisure and Recreation

(1) The 50-plus age groups will be recognized as growing markets for recreation goods and services.

(2) Leisure opportunities for women, both married and single, will be more diverse and less tied to the family.

(3) The increasing size of the "new class" with discretionary income and more education will attract disproportionate attention from those planning for recreation programs and provisions, especially in the market sector.

(4) Major attention will have to be given to "off hour" employment and the potential for recreation participation during weekdays and at odd times, especially by those employed in the service sector of the economy.

(5) Sunset or declining activities will balance sunrise recreation. For example, the basis of hunting seems to be shrinking at the same time that backpacking is growing. Again, education levels as well as urbanization are factors in such changing tastes.

(6) More and more adults at any one time are either single or in a period of transition. Leisure settings and opportunities will increase for those who do not come in couples or families. Singleness will be accepted as a more common and less extraordinary mode of life, whether temporary or relatively permanent.

(7) The business sector will become more central to recreation provisions. And the complementary nature of market and public sector resources and programs will become increasingly significant.

(8) Space scarcities will become more acute, especially in prime environments such as national parks, major museums, and urban facilities. The urban space crunch will be intensified by more multiple-unit housing and the decline of the private residential yard.

(9) Home electronic entertainments will become more diverse and less costly. Those technologies that are compatible with current lifetyles will gain enormous markets and increase the attraction of at-home entertainment. For the foreseeable future, interactive formats and games will continue to be marginal to most leisure styles.

(10) The diversity in life and leisure styles will continue despite the power of mass marketing. In fact, many "market segments" will be identified more by their leisure styles than by economic factors.

(11) Concentration on the "high end" for leisure businesses will saturate the market and cause business failures. Middle mass markets may become recognized for more kinds of businesses. In the meantime, however, the imbalance of opportunities for the affluent will intensify.

(12) Reduced public subsidies in areas such as the arts and outdoor resources will open many possible markets for businesses and diversify programs for the public resources. Reliance on cost recovery will tend to raise user fees for further public provisions even further.

(13) The higher activity levels and greater financial resources of the retired will bring increased attention to the "active old" as recreation participants.

(14) New technologies will impact on particular activities much as fiberglass did on boating and skiing. Such technologies are extremely important when they lower the costs or reduce the pain of acquiring enough skill to gain satisfaction from the activity.

(15) Nonfamily leisure settings and organization will become more and more important due to demographic changes and the long postparental period of the family life cycle.

(16)   Travel provisions will become more varied to accommodate various styles. Packages will be more diverse and almost any amenity will be available for rent.

(17) "Big toys" will be purchased by some. At the same time, however, some highly educated adults will avoid being tied down to particular locales or equipment. They will seek variety by refusing the big-ticket purchases. The "special use" car as a personal expression will become increasingly common with its allure of possession and symbol of individuality.

(18) The skills associated with recreation will become more important as more individuals define themselves and their competence in terms of what they can do and accomplish off the job. As a result, provisions for enhancing skills at levels above "beginner" will grow in public and market sector programs. At the same time, gains in skills will create new demand for programs and resources.

(19)   Employed women will be recognized as a market opportunity almost equal to men. Over time the established bias toward male programs and provisions will almost disappear.

How will all these continuities and changes meld into a varied but integrated whole? There are too many dimensions of change to produce a neat picture of the future. Much more is possible than this century will see. Nevertheless, it is important to try to keep such general continuities and changes in mind as we focus on particular activities and contexts.

38

References:

Ehrenreich, Barbara. 1986. Is The Middle Class Doomed? *New York Times Magazine.* September 7.

Fromm, Erich. 1955. *The Sane Society.* New York: Holt, Rinehart, and Winston.

Fuchs, Victor. 1983. *How We Live: an Economic Perspective on Americans from Birth to Death.* Cambridge: Harvard University Press.

Kelly, John R. 1987. *Peoria Winter: Later Life Styles and Resources.* Boston: Lexington Books. D. C. Heath.

Maslow, Abraham. 1954. Hierarchy of Human Needs, in *Motivation and Personality.* New York: Harper and Row.

Masnick, George, and Mary Jo Bane. 1980. *The Nation's Families: 1960-1990.* (Cambridge: Harvard-MIT Joint Center for Urban Studies).

Mediamark Research, Inc. 1986. *Leisurestyles.* New York.

Mitchell, Arnold. 1983. *The Nine American Lifestyles.* New York: Warner Books.

Riesman, David, 1950. *The Lonely Crowd: a Study of the Changing American Character.* New Haven: Yale University Press.

RECREATION PROJECTIONS: INTRODUCTION

Projections will be presented in the next chapters under three general categories of activities:

Chapter 3: Recreation in Natural Resource Environments

Chapter 4: Recreation in Community Settings

Chapter 5: At-home Recreation

Each chapter will include two levels of analysis. Eighteen activities will include relatively complete analyses of long-term and short-term trends, participation by age cohorts, and "target markets." Less trend data are available for another 21 activities. Analysis for them will consist of a more concise review of current participation and particularly significant market segments.

Sources of Data

The limitations of the data base were outlined in Chapter 1. Even the series of national outdoor recreation surveys is not comparable in samples, instrumentation, or measurement. The Neilsen survey lasted less than ten years and ended in 1983. The two market surveys moved slowly into recreation with a small number of activities in 1976 and gradual additions in the next decade. Further, data from the Neilsen survey can only be released for general use a year after publication for clients who require confidentiality. Breakdowns by age, gender, and income level are now available only for the later national surveys. Moreover, the categories of activities have changed. For example, in some surveys, camping in developed areas is now distinguished from camping in dispersed sites, beach and lake swimming is distinguished from pool swimming, and distance running is distinguished from jogging. Earlier data aggregates such differences and requires judicious estimates of the types and styles of participation.

The data employed in the trend analysis and projections of this study are:

(1) *NRS* - The National Recreation Surveys of 1965 and 1983. Sample sizes: 1965 = 7,194 and 1983 = 5,757.

(2) *ACN* - The A. C. Nielsen Sports Market Surveys of 1973, 1976, 1979, and 1982. The numbers of individual participants in the thousands were projected from a sample of 3,000 households.

(3) *SMS* - The Simmons Market Share Survey from 1976 to 1985 with a national sample of over 15,000 households.

(4) *MRI* - The Mediamark Research, Inc., national survey of 1984 with a national sample of over 20,000 households.

The participation trend graphs combine sources of data when viable. The percentages are rounded to the nearest tenth of a percent, but they should not be treated as precise and absolute. There is considerable consistency among the sources when measurement differences are recognized. It is the overall trends, however, that we are seeking here. Exact percentages are subject to enough error that differences of 2 or 3 percent should not be given much weight. Year-to-year figures on gender and age differences and trends are, on the other hand, quite consistent and reliable.

Analysis Format

For each full analysis, the following format will be employed:

(1) Longer-term trends when available.

(2) Trends since 1975 and projections to the year 2000.

(3) Use of age data to engage in cohort analysis and projections.

(4) Identification of target markets.

(5) Future projections.

Target Market Identification

The market segments will be evaluated in one of four categories:

G = "Growth market" for which there is evidence of continued increasing participation during the next fifteen years.

E = "Established market" which is currently significant, but will likely remain relatively stable.

P = "Potential market," now of modest size, but with indications of future growth.

L = "Low probability market" for which demand is expected to remain relatively low.

Demand segments or target markets will be identified according to two dimensions: life course and socio-economic position.

Life Course Periods

The life course does not always proceed without disruption. A recent study found that about 60 percent of adults over age 40 had experienced either a major turning point or a series of disruptions requiring significant change in order to cope (Kelly, 1987). Further, periods of the life course are not sharply disjunctive. Rather, the transitions are anticipated and tend to be relatively smooth for most making their life journeys. Nevertheless, life course period does identify common role expectations in work and family as well as shifts in access to resources and developmental aims. The following life course categories will be employed in our analysis:

(1) "Preparation." The period of young adulthood in which school and work engagements are still geared toward later commitments and careers. It is a time of exploration in which many role expectations are still relatively open.

(2) "Free singles." The period in which work roles are being inaugurated, but marriage and family commitments are still in the future. It is a period for seeking intimacy and relatedness in which leisure is oriented toward both personal development and exploring relationships. There is also an intermediate state for couples who have made a commitment to each other, but have not yet begun childbearing and childrearing.

(3) "Young parents." The transition to parenting has drastic impacts on time and money resources, aims for recreation, the use of space, and work career trajectories. Increasingly the marriage commitment is now tied to a decision to have children, usually no more than two and in a brief period.

(4) "Establishment." The period of productivity in work, family, and community. Commitments to work, family, and other salient roles are at a peak. Resources are allocated in ways that

enhance and express these commitments. It is, for most adults, generally coincident with the time children are in school.

(5) "Transitionals." For a high proportion of adults, the time of parenting and establishment is interrupted by change. Marriages dissolve, work careers are diverted or ended, and other traumas impact life. Therefore, more and more adults at any one time are in a period of transition rather than stability.

(6) "Late singles." Such transitions will be resolved for many by re-entry into established work and family roles. For others, however, singleness will become more permanent. They will be adult singles, with or without parenting responsibilities, who will not have the context of a stable marriage or other intimate relationship.

(7) "Pre-retirement adults." Their children are more or less out of the home and on their own. They may be at the peak of their earnings curve and have more freedom to allocate time than in any period of their lives. Further, they often are assessing their priorities and making changes based on what they want for the remainder of their lives. As a consequence, they are a prime market for many kinds of recreation provisions.

(8) "Active oldsters." They are in the earlier retirement period, yet retain reasonable health and competence for activity. Each cohort entering this period has been equipped with a more adequate income and higher education background than the one previous. They have expectations for a satisfying life period and usually believe that they have earned the right to enjoy themselves.

(9) "The frail." Those in the final period of life with limited abilities and resources. Their lives have often become constricted in social circles, geography, and range of activities. Their recreation is usually home-centered.

Resource-based Categories

Recreation participation requires resources of time, skill, and usually financial cost. These resources vary through the life course, but even more according to one's place in the social system. Individuals may be categorized variously according to their general access to social and economic resources. Since our focus is on target markets for recreation by life course period, four categories will be employed, based primarily on amount and source of income. These economic factors are usually consistent with type and stability of employment and education preparation.

(1) "Low-end markets." The poor and those with marginal incomes and employment. They may move in and out of arbitrary "poverty" classifications but are never far from exhausting their very limited resources.

(2) "Middle-mass markets." With more stable employment that has very limited potential for advancement, the middle mass includes those working in factory, office, retailing, and other jobs where replacements are nearly always available. Nevertheless, many are buying homes, have adequate transportation, take a little vacation, engage in low-cost recreation, and often hope their children can go to college somewhere.

(3) "Discretionaries." The key to recreation spending is "discretionary income," a level that permits the allocation of a consistent and substantial portion to leisure including travel, equipment, skill-acquisition, and special events. They may be in any life course period, but their aims change in relation to their social roles and expectations. They are most likely to be "actives" in the Mediamark Leisurestyles scheme.

(4) "High-end market." The 5 percent or so who possess wealth. They make major leisure purchases, rent or buy especially attractive environments, travel far and often, and are the target for many high-investment kinds of recreation provisions. Recreation for them is often tied to real estate investments and travel to destinations where numbers are limited by costs.

The sizes of these four socio-economic segments can be calculated in several ways. In general, the "low-end market" comprises 15 to 20 percent of households in the United States, "middle mass" approximately 35 to 45 percent, "discretionaries" about 30 to 35 percent, and the "high end" 5 to 10 percent of the total. Of course they are not discrete categories. Many households fall into the "cracks" with some characteristics of two classifications. Educated young parents, for example, have the social characteristics of "discretionaries," but often have the financial constraints of the "middle mass."

A "Target Market Finder" display will be offered for those activities with significant participation rates and for which the data base is adequate to the analysis.

Reference:

Kelly, John R. 1987. *Peoria Winter: Later Life Styles and Resources.* Boston: Lexington Books, D.C. Heath.

RECREATION IN
NATURAL RESOURCE
ENVIRONMENTS

This chapter contains participation trends and analyses for activities that require natural resource environments. For some, a significant element of the activity is immersion in the environment. The forest, water, or mountain itself is at the center of the experience. For others, the resource simply makes the activity possible. The activities are not all "outdoor recreation," but those that call for access to special natural resources.

For many participants, natural resource-based recreation requires travel to the special environment. As a consequence, some participation is occasional, possible only during vacations or other blocks of time. Activities such as backpacking or downhill skiing may be reserved for a once-a-year special trip. Frequency figures do not necessarily reflect commitment to the activity as they tend to do for community-based activity. Further, costs of participation may be quite high when they include travel, lodging, food, and foregone income as well as direct costs of participation. Individuals may save and plan for months for a once-a-year event that punctuates the more routine engagements of the remainder of the year.

At the same time, participants who live close to the lake or forest can engage in the activity almost any day in season. They may sail or cross-country ski as frequently as others walk. The statistics cannot take into account access and travel costs, so they mix participants for whom access is costly with those who can walk to the resource.

There are also significant climatic differences. Activities restricted to a single season in some parts of the country are possible year-round in others. Again, travel may allow some to participate during their local off-season. But this kind of adaptation tends to be restricted to the high-end markets and a few devotees who make extraordinary arrangements.

Thus markets for many resource-based activities differ considerably from region to region. Hiking possibilities and timetables are quite different from Oregon to Indiana. The ecology of skiing varies widely from Colorado to Illinois to Florida. Sailing is seasonal but geographically accessible in Michigan, year-round but ecologically limited in Arizona. The national trends may not accurately reflect participation patterns in a specific locale.

BACKPACKING AND HIKING

The older surveys included only "hiking" as an activity category. Therefore, we have no comparable long-term data on backpacking. More recent surveys have combined backpacking and hiking so that such resource-based activity is clearly distinguished from more prosaic walking. Only in 1985 did the SMS market survey distinguish hiking from backpacking.

Long-term trends

The NRS comparison indicates a dramatic increase in "hiking" participation from 1965 to 1983.

Participation in backpacking in 1983, however, was 6 percent for males and 3 percent for females. This suggests that

Participation by Gender			
Year	Male	Female	Total
1965	7	5	6
1983	15	13	14

day hiking is about four times more common than hiking that requires packing in overnight equipment.

The most dramatic long-term change is for those over age 25. Hiking and backpacking are less confined to youth and young adults even though participation rates drop significantly for each older age category.

The long-term trend, therefore, is one of dramatic increase, primarily in the adult age categories. This suggests that these cohorts will continue to participate in hiking at higher rates as they move through the life course.

Participation by Age		
Age	1965	1983
18 to 24	18	19
25 to 39	10	17
40 to 59	6	12
60+	1	5

Short-term trends

The short-term trends are somewhat obscured in the Simmons Survey by changes in the activity categories. Adjustment for the change, however, reveals a moderate but consistent upward curve in participation. Comparison with the MRI data supports this trend, although the MRI percentages are 50 percent lower than the SMS.

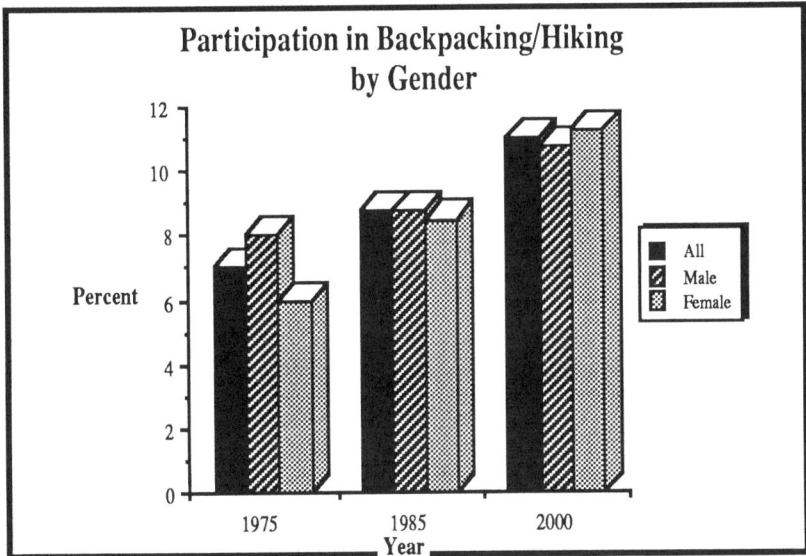

Participation in Backpacking/Hiking by Gender

SMS indicates that about 40 percent of those who hiked or backpacked did so at least ten times a year. About a third hiked less than four times and only about 3 percent hiked more than 25 times a year. The MRI breakdown is similar: 18 percent hiked more than ten times a year. In general, backpacking tends to be a special event and for many participants only once a year. In 1985, 40 percent of those participating did so one to four times and 65 percent did go less than ten times. Hiking, however, may be more frequent, less bound to special environments, and sometimes even just a preparation for a long overnight trek.

48

Cohort analysis

The bar graph on participation by age shows that hiking and backpacking are strongly related to age. Even though the long-term rates for older adults increased dramatically, in 1985 the participation rate for those over age 55 was only half that of those under age 35. Markets for hiking do not disappear for those in pre-retirement and even active retirement, however.

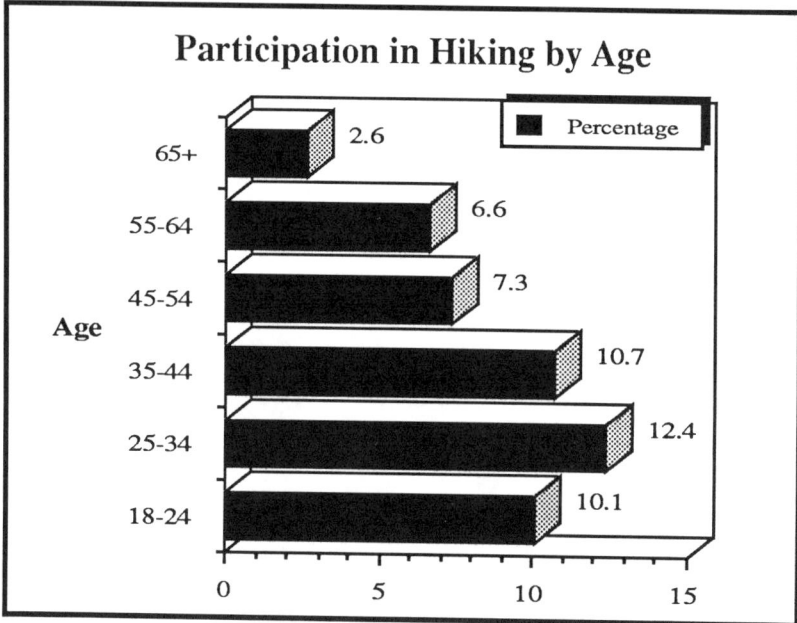

Participation in Hiking by Age

Age	Percentage
65+	2.6
55-64	6.6
45-54	7.3
35-44	10.7
25-34	12.4
18-24	10.1

Age is also a factor in backpacking. In the 1985 SMS survey, backpacking rates were 2.9 percent for those age 18 to 24, 2.8 percent for those age 25 to 34, 1.6 percent for those age 35 to 44, 1.2 percent for those age 45 to 54, 1.4 percent for those age 55 to 64, and 0.3 percent for those age 65 and over. The lack of significant fall-off from ages 35 to 64 indicates that those who are dedicated to backpacking are likely to continue throughout the active years of the life course.

Target markets

Other dimensions of market segmentation also suggest disparate participation. Gender differences are now slight for hiking, while for backpacking, about twice as many males as females participate: 2.5 percent for males versus 1.2 percent for females. Education and income are significant predictors even though hiking may be a low-cost activity.

Participation by Education Levels

Education level	Hiking	Backpacking
Less than high school	4.9	.6
High school grad	7.3	1.8
Some college	11.8	2.5
College grad	14.8	2.8

Income yields a similar rate of increase that reflects the travel costs of some hiking as well as taste differences. Backpacking, however, is less related to income, perhaps because of the student and young adult cohorts:

Participation by Income Levels

Income level	Hiking	Backpacking
-$10,000	5.0	1.2
$10 to 24,999	7.4	1.7
$25 to 34,999	11.5	2.1
$35 to 49,999	11.3	2.3

Note that participation levels are the same from middle to high income categories. Hiking and backpacking, then, are relatively infrequent for low-income households, but are no more common at the high-end than for moderate-income households.

Target markets for hiking and backpacking range in age from youth to active retirees and include both men and women. Special attention may be given to middle-income adults who have some college education. Further, styles of hiking and backpacking may be quite different for the Discretionaries who would be most likely to focus on special environments and to obtain special equipment. Young Discretionaries are the prime target market for backpacking since it requires physical conditioning, equipment, and select environments.

50

RECREATION TARGET MARKETS: BACKPACKING/HIKING			

G = GROWTH MARKET   P = POTENTIAL MARKET
E = ESTABLISHED MARKET   L = LOW-PROBABILITY MARKET

Category	Low-end	Middle Mass	Discretionaries	High-end
Preparation	P	P	G	G
Free singles	L	P	G	G
Young parents	L	P	P	L
Established	L	E	E	L
Transitionals	L	P	P	P
Late singles	L	P	G	P
Preretirement	L	P	G	P
Active oldsters	L	P	P	L
The frail	L	L	L	L

Future projections

Hiking and backpacking projections should be divided between local hiking and hiking and backpacking that involves special environments and equipment. Local hiking varies from region to region. Projection of current trends would suggest a gradual increase in participation, especially among cohorts who will be in their 40s, 50s, and 60s. The trend appears quite solid and broad enough to support an increased demand for opportunities and equipment.

Backpacking is more select. Target markets are more concentrated on the younger age segments with at least some college education. The general need to travel to special locales for overnight hiking adds an economic element to choices. Equipment options and styles of back-country camping, however, vary widely in cost. Student-age participants often find relatively low-cost ways of backpacking. Families with younger children, on the other hand, generally are restricted to day hiking from more established base camps. Backpacking most often takes place on public lands and depends on management policies that open those lands, maintain trails, and promote safety.

BOATING: POWERBOATING

Powerboating includes several styles of participation. Some boating is "cruiser style" and involves boats with cabins, cooking facilities, and other amenities. Some powerboating is primarily for waterskiing and requires speed and power. Some is more environmental, based on floating platforms or even houseboats. Some supports fishing, whether in fresh-water lakes and streams or in salt water. The data do not distinguish such orientations and styles. Waterskiing and fishing, however, are analyzed separately. This section focuses on participation that is self-identified as "boating."

Long-term trends

The NRS surveys indicate insignificant increases in boating participation from 1965 to 1983, from 31 percent to 32 percent for males and from 22 percent to 24 percent for females. The Nielsen surveys, however, report a consistent growth trend with increases of 8 percent from 1973 to 1976, another 8 percent from 1976 to 1979, and 11 percent from 1979 to 1983. These increases reflect both the growth in adult population and increases in cost-adjusted income for most of that period. The participation figures do not measure changes in frequency and style or in levels of expenditure. All boating is aggregated rather than separating powerboating from canoeing and other forms. The figures do suggest, however, that even with the impacts of fiberglass and economic growth, boating participation has remained more stable than might have been anticipated. Markets have grown in proportion to the population rather than in disproportionate leaps.

Short-term trends

In 1979, the SMS surveys started to differentiate power-boating from other forms. The short-term trend for the period 1979 to 1985 is one of gradual decline from 8.1 percent of the adult population in 1979 to 6.7 percent in 1985. Further, only about 40 percent of the participants engage in powerboating more than ten times a year.

Participation in Powerboating by Gender

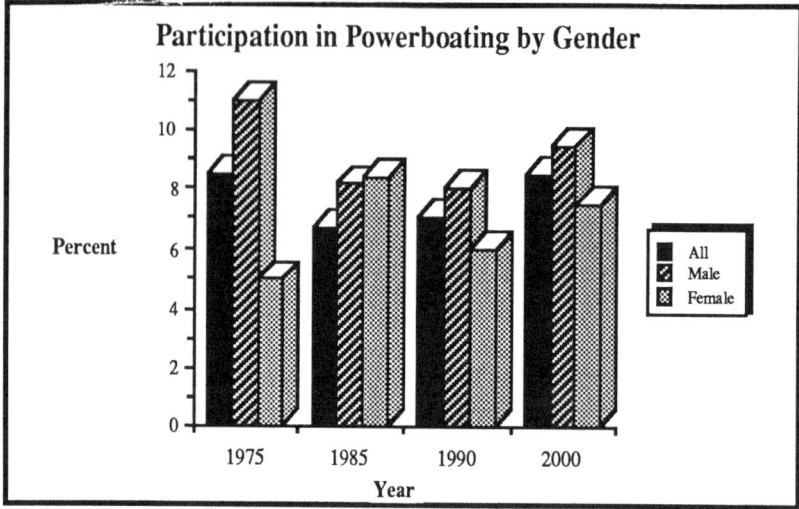

A number of factors may underlie this slight decline. First, the gas crises caused some shift away from fuel-intensive boating during the period of escalating prices and supply uncertainties. Second, much powerboating is cost-intensive so that the markets are limited. Overnight cruising, for example, is clearly restricted to high-end markets. Third, storage and mooring spaces are limited, especially near major cities. Fourth, access to good boating opportunities is uneven and limited to certain regions. Fifth, even where there is water, climate restricts the season in northern areas. Sixth, some people just are not comfortable on or around the water. In short, environmental and cost factors limit the potential markets for powerboating.

Cohort analysis

Powerboating is not a strongly age-related activity unless we differentiate styles of use. Cruising is more common for older families and adults, while water-skiing is restricted largely to those under age 30. For the generic category of activity, somewhat lower rates of participation are found for those over age 45 with a sharp drop for those aged 65 and over.

The SMS survey, however, has an unusual component. The 2.9 percent who engage in powerboating over ten times a year actually peaks at 4 percent for the 45 to 54 age group and remains

Participation in Powerboating by Age

Age	Percentage
65+	2.2
55-64	4.2
45-54	5.8
35-44	8.8
25-34	8.7
18-24	8.6

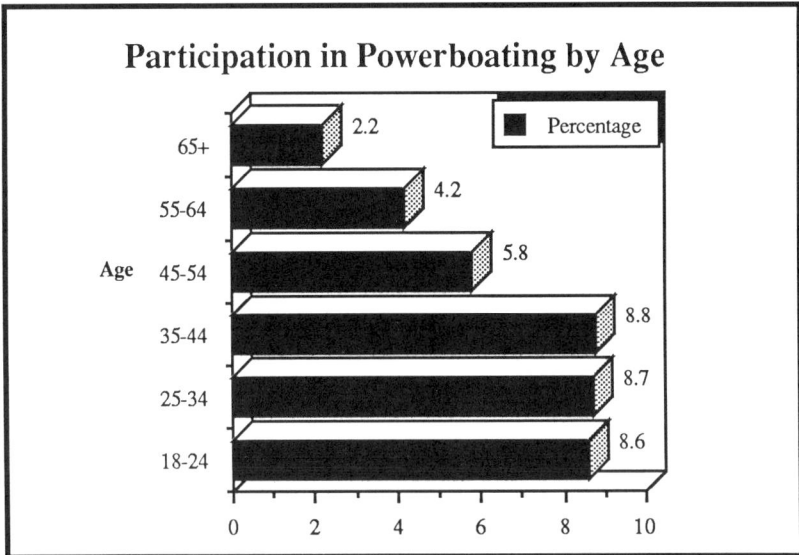

at 2.5 percent for those aged 55 to 64. Regular powerboating, then, is inversely related to age up to retirement level. This suggests that the current cohorts in their 20s and 30s may have relatively high rates of participation when they are in their 40s, 50s, and even 60s. The long-term future rates of powerboating may well reverse the more recent decline.

Target markets

Participation By Income

Household income	Percentage
-$10,000	2.0
$10 to 24,999	5.0
$25 to 34,999	10.1
$35 to 49,999	10.5
$50,000+	11.8

Powerboating is strongly related to income. It is a cost-intensive activity.

Income more than education is predictive of powerboating activity. Gender differences are significant, but both men and women are important in the market segmentation. High-end participants are THE main market for costly yachts and cruisers. Discretionaries engage in more varied styles of boating. While there is some concern over power versus nonpower styles of boating related to the lifestyles of well-educated Discretionaries, they remain the greatest potential market, especially as the "boomers" move into their late 30s, 40s, and 50s.

RECREATION TARGET MARKETS: POWERBOATING				
G = GROWTH MARKET P = POTENTIAL MARKET E = ESTABLISHED MARKET L = LOW-PROBABILITY MARKET				
Category	Low-end	Middle Mass	Discretionaries	High-end
Preparation	L	L	L	P
Free singles	L	P	P	G
Young parents	L	L	L	P
Established	L	P	G	G
Transitionals	L	L	P	P
Late singles	L	P	P	P
Preretirement	L	P	G	G
Active oldsters	L	L	P	P
The frail	L	L	L	L

The Middle mass is a viable market for boats related to fresh-water fishing and other less costly styles.

Future projections

Despite recent trends of small declines in powerboating participation, a reversal is quite possible. The impacts of the energy crisis will decline over time. Most important is the established lack of age-related decline in powerboating: those most committed are disproportionately High-end and Discretionary adults in their 40s and 50s, just the age that will increase in size through this century. If access to water and facilities for boat launching, mooring, and storage can grow with the potential demand, then some gradual increase in participation may occur in the remainder of the century. One problematic issue, however, is competition from nonpower boating such as sailing, canoeing, and kayaking. These styles are more consistent with an environmental ethic and with interests in health and more strenuous activity.

CAMPING

Camping, like so many other recreation activities, includes a wide variety of participation styles. Federal agencies now distinguish between "developed-area" and "dispersed" camping. Within the same campgrounds are campers with simple tents, tent trailers, small trailers, elaborate trailers requiring special towing vehicles, camping units on pick-up trucks, and self-contained mobile "homes." Campers enter the forests and deserts alone and in groups. The groups may consist of nuclear families, young couples, friends, or members of an organization. The camping may be a means to gain access to a special resource such as a beach, river, or rock face; or the experience of camping itself may be primary. Some camp to save money while traveling and others to get into an attractive environment. The SMS survey reports that of the 18.4 percent of the adult population who camped in 1984, 15 percent used a truck-mounted camper, 10 percent used mobile homes, 18 percent used towable trailers, 10 percent used towable folding tent trailers, and 6 percent used converted van campers. Almost half, then, still camp with some form of tent or portable shelter.

In most market surveys this is all called "camping." The trends do not distinguish shifts in styles of camping. To some extent, those styles can be estimated by age categories, family status, and income. Camping, however, may involve elaborate equipment for those of moderate incomes and be quite spartan for those who seek simplicity and detachment from "civilization."

Long-term trends

The National Recreation surveys indicate long-term growth in participation. This is consistent with figures on campground use gathered by federal and state agencies. Although the 1983 national survey figures may be inflated, there are many indications that participation in camping increased steadily during the 1960s and 70s. Equipment purchases increased. Market-sector provisions in both campground chains and local businesses were developed. In some areas, private campgrounds sold sites on which owners placed trailers to be used as second homes.

The NRS indicates increases for men from 11 percent in 1965 to 28 percent in 1983 and for women from 8 percent to 22 percent. The Nielsen data are more consistent with current market surveys. ACN shows increases of 7 percent from 1973 to 1976, 4 percent from 1976 to 1979, and 2 percent from 1979 to 1982. This trend of growth at a decreasing rate drops to stability for the percentage of adults who camped in the 1980s.

The long-term general trend seems to be one of a steady increase in camping participation from 1965 into the 1980s, but with the rate of increase dropping to stability. Obscured by this general trend, however, is the development of more variety in styles and equipment. In 1965, most camping involved a tent carried in a family car. By 1980, camping ranged from ultralight carry-in tents and food to mobile homes with two bedrooms, two baths, two televisions, and a VCR.

Short-term trends

The SMS surveys indicate a slight reduction in the proportion of American adults who did any camping in the 1980s. The drop is also consistent for those who camped fifteen times or more during the year and for all age and income categories.

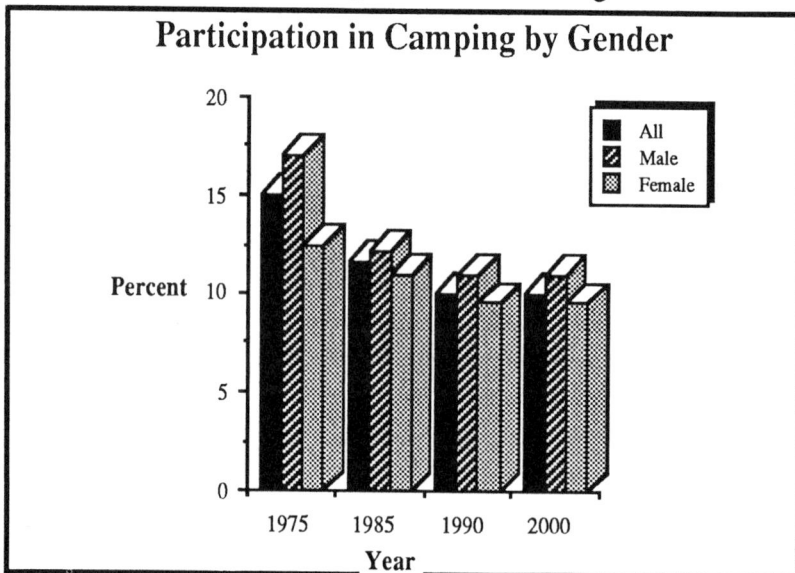

Participation in Camping by Gender

In the Simmons survey, frequency figures suggest that camping is an occasional event for most. Of the total of 11.6 percent of adults who camped in 1985, 7.9 percent (65 percent of the total campers) were camping ten days or less, 2.9 percent camped 11 to 24 days, 0.5 percent camped 25 to 59 days, and 0.3 percent camped 60 days or more. In the MRI survey for 1984, 60 percent of those who camped took only one or two trips. Most campers do so once or twice a summer rather than any more regularly.

Overall then, there seems to have been a trend toward increased camping participation that leveled off after 1975 with a period of slight decrease during the 1980s.

Cohort Analysis

Camping is not limited to any elite groups in the society. The gender difference has been narrowing. Although those over age 35 camp less than those in their teens and 20s, there is a sizable cohort of campers through preretirement and even into retirement years. In fact, the Active oldsters are a significant portion of the market for comfortable camping equipment.

The same spread is the case for education and income variables. Only those at poverty levels and those who have not completed high school camp at lower rates. Camping would appear to be as much a Middle mass as upper income activity:

Target markets and the future

Demand for camping opportunities is dispersed across the adult population with significant markets in almost every socio-economic category.

Participation by Income 1985	
Income	% Camping
-$10,000	4.9
$10 to 24,999	11.5
$25 to 34,999	14.5
$35 to 49,999	14.4
$50,000+	13.9

Moreover, the age cohorts that are growing — the established, preretirement, and retirement adults — can be expected to be able to continue to make significant investments in camping. Although the period of rapid growth may be over, camping has

Participation by Education	
Education	% Camping
Less than HS grad	6.2
HS grad	12.6
Some college	14.8
College grad	13.8

solid markets. Further, research into camping styles according to income level and period in the life course could identify markets for particular resources and types of equipment.

RECREATION TARGET MARKETS: CAMPING

G = GROWTH MARKET   P = POTENTIAL MARKET
E = ESTABLISHED MARKET   L = LOW-PROBABILITY MARKET

Category	Low-end	Middle Mass	Discretionaries	High-end
Preparation	L	P	E	P
Free singles	L	P	P	P
Young parents	L	E	E	E
Established	L	E	E	E
Transitionals	L	L	L	L
Late singles	L	P	P	P
Preretirement	L	G	G	P
Active oldsters	L	P	P	L
The frail	L	L	L	L

FISHING

Fishing, too, is characterized by a variety of styles. The types of water, fish, equipment, and access differ widely. Some back-country trout fishing with flycasting equipment involves considerable hiking and often camping. At the other extreme are large cruise boat excursions with professional crews seeking very large "trophy" fish. Different people fish in the same water for the same fish from boats, piers, or the banks, with sport aims or food aims, and with sophisticated casting rods and reels or simple poles and worms. The older data sources label all this as "fishing." One current market study divides fishing into salt water and fresh water and fly and other fishing.

Long-term trends

The National Recreation surveys indicate measured growth in fishing from 1965 to 1983: from 41 percent to 47 percent for men and 20 percent to 23 percent for women. The Nielsen sports survey is inconsistent for the 1973 to 1983 period: a 4 percent gain from 1973 to 1976, a 7 percent loss from 1976 to 1979, and a 7 percent gain from 1979 to 1983.

Probable participation trends since World War II appear to parallel those of other resource-based activities. A significant increase in participation during the 1970s was followed by a slowing rate of growth and overall stability in the 1980s.

Short-term trends

The market surveys support the latter part of this estimate. SMS indicates a major drop in participation from 1976 to 1983 with the likelihood of a decreasing rate of decline. The decline in participation appears to be consistent across age, income, and education categories with the following exceptions:

- The 18- to 24-year-old category decreased 15 percent from 1982 to 1985.
- The 35- to 44-year-old age group increased 9 percent in participation from 1982 to 1985.
- The decrease from 1982 to 1985 was almost entirely among those of lower education levels.

The styles of fishing that are most likely to have increased participation may be those consistent with the lifestyles of more

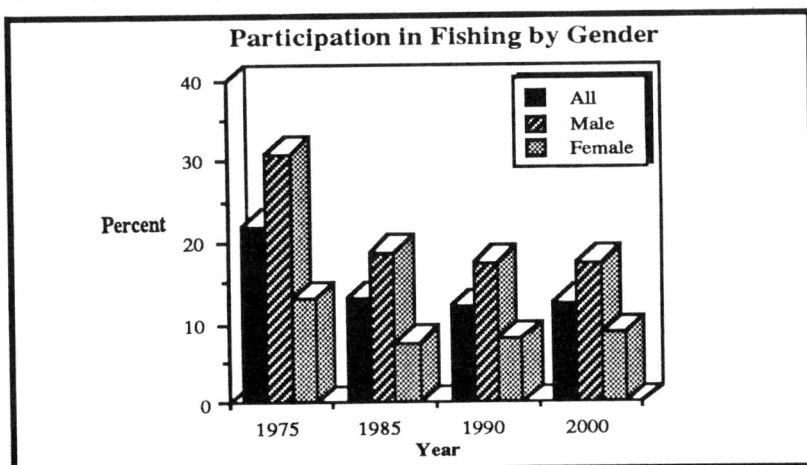

Participation in Fishing by Gender

established adults, that is those of middle income and in the childrearing period of the life course.

Frequency figures suggest that most of those who fish do so rarely. Of the 13 percent of the adult population who claim to have fished in 1985 (SMS), 3.8 percent did so only one to four times, 3.1 percent did so five to nine times, 4.2 percent did so 10 to 24 times, and 1.9 percent did so 25 times or more. Fishing appears to be a classic "20-80" activity in which 20 percent of the participants provide 80 percent of the total demand. The MRI 1984 survey found that two-thirds or those who fished did so less than twelve days during the year.

Cohort analysis

Fishing is an activity that most devotees expect to continue well into retirement. Age breakdowns suggest that this hope is somewhat optimistic, but not entirely unfounded. Fishing is as much an activity for those in midlife as for the young. Only in the late 50s does the drop-off in participating become marked. Further, even for those aged 65 and older, the rate is about 40 percent that of the adult total.

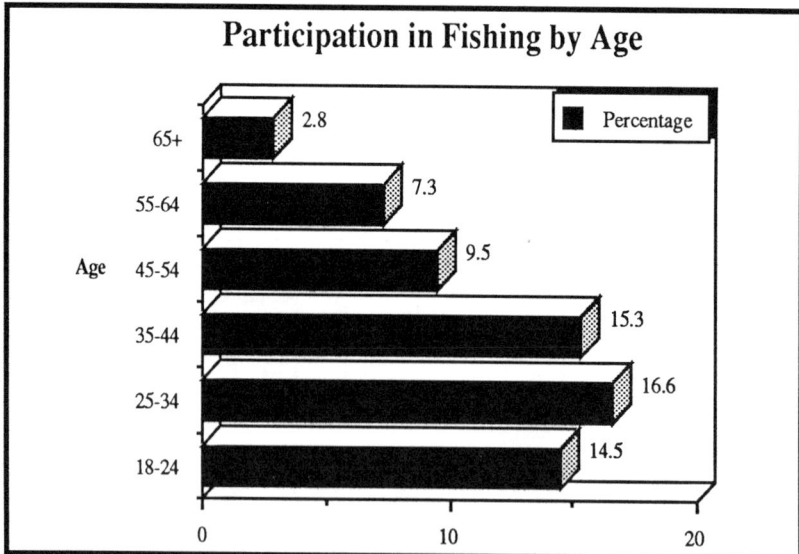

Participation in Fishing by Age

Age	Percentage
65+	2.8
55-64	7.3
45-54	9.5
35-44	15.3
25-34	16.6
18-24	14.5

The most intriguing age-related finding is that rates are almost exactly the same from age 25 to 45. Fishing is an activity with a lengthy life course appeal. In fact, more than any outdoor activity except golf, fishing is an activity for the full life span up to frailty. It has the potential for stability as the population ages.

Target markets

The possibilties of continuing fishing through most of the adult life course points to the importance of established, pre-retirement and active oldster markets. The gender difference, in which women are less than half as likely to fish as men, is not likely to change.

Fishing is a Middle Mass phenomenon. The rates are highest for men with some college education but without degrees. Over the years, those with incomes under $25,000 have been slightly more likely to fish than those with middle or higher incomes. Fishing is not a highly segmented activity. The markets are quite general and spread across the population. Access to locales would seem to be more determinative than age or socio-economic factors.

RECREATION TARGET MARKETS: FISHING				
G = GROWTH MARKET P = POTENTIAL MARKET E = ESTABLISHED MARKET L = LOW-PROBABILITY MARKET				
Category	Low-end	Middle Mass	Discretionaries	High-end
Preparation	E	E	E	E
Free singles	E	E	E	E
Young parents	E	E	E	E
Established	E	G	G	E
Transitionals	P	E	L	L
Late singles	L	E	L	L
Preretirement	E	P	P	P
Active oldsters	L	E	E	P
The frail	L	L	L	L

Future projections

It appears that fishing participation will be very stable throughout this century. The markets are only moderately segmented and identified. It is an activity with wide appeal, at least for men. There are, however, two conflicting elements: the "boomer" cohort is now the one most likely to fish; and fishing is less common among those with higher education levels. These growing market segments may just about cancel each other out. The other negative element in the projection is that those aged 18 to 24 show the greatest reductions in participation. If due to ongoing urbanization, then a long-term decline in participation may be projected for the activity, mitigated only by the boomer cohort in the next decade.

Participation in Various Types of Fishing

Age	Salt water	Flycasting	Other fresh water
18 to 24	4.0	3.5	13.7
25 to 34	5.3	4.0	16.8
35 to 44	5.3	2.7	15.1
45 to 54	5.0	2.1	11.8
55 to 64	4.0	2.5	10.6
65+	2.2	1.9	6.9
Gender			
Male	6.4	4.5	18.8
Female	2.6	1.5	7.8
Total	4.4	2.9	13.0

Specialized Types of Fishing

The 1985 SMS survey identifies three kinds of fishing. The varying rates of participation for the three give a general picture of the relative significance of each.

Salt water fishing is most correlated with income levels and fly-casting is somewhat less. Other types of fresh-water fishing have the highest participation rates in the middle income ranges. All three types of fishing are gender-differentiated. The market for salt water fishing is not related to age up to age 65. Fly fishing, on the other hand, drops around age 35 and then a stable level is maintained into retirement years. It would seem that those who become committed to this skill-oriented kind of fishing maintain their engagement through the life span. As might be expected, the specialized types of fishing show higher levels of commitment and greater lifetime consistency.

HUNTING

Hunting is one of the least complex recreation activities in styles of participation and in composition of participants. It is the most clearly gender-differentiated outdoor recreation activity, with a socialization pattern of being passed on from father to son. Its environments are rural, but hunters come from all kinds of communities. In some cases they travel considerable distances to engage in the activity, usually in company with other men.

Long-term trends

Both sources of long-term data on hunting indicate a decline in participation. The NRS shows a reduction from 25 percent to 22 percent for men from 1965 to 1983 with women registering an increase from 2 percent to 3 percent. All the reduction is among males between the ages of 12 and 24, from 19 percent to 15 percent. Increased urbanization and other factors seem to have reduced the number of males being introduced to hunting.

The Nielsen sports survey indicates a 4 percent increase in the number of participants between 1973 and 1976 followed by a 4 percent drop in the period 1976 to 1979 and a 5 percent drop between 1979 and 1982. A period of small growth in the number of hunters occurred when the "boomer" cohort entered their teens. Again, there seems to be a steady, if unspectacular, reduction in hunting participation through the 1970s and into the 80s.

Short-term trends

The SMS surveys indicate a dramatic reduction in hunting activity between 1979 and 1982 — for males, from 19 percent to 13.9 percent. Again, almost all the loss occurred in the younger age categories: from 13.5 percent to 8.7 percent for those aged 18 to 24 and from 9.7 percent to 8.5 percent for those aged 25 to 34.

On the other hand, the next cohorts, aged 35 to 44 and 45 to 54, each increased about 1.5 percent in hunting participation.

Participation in Hunting by Gender

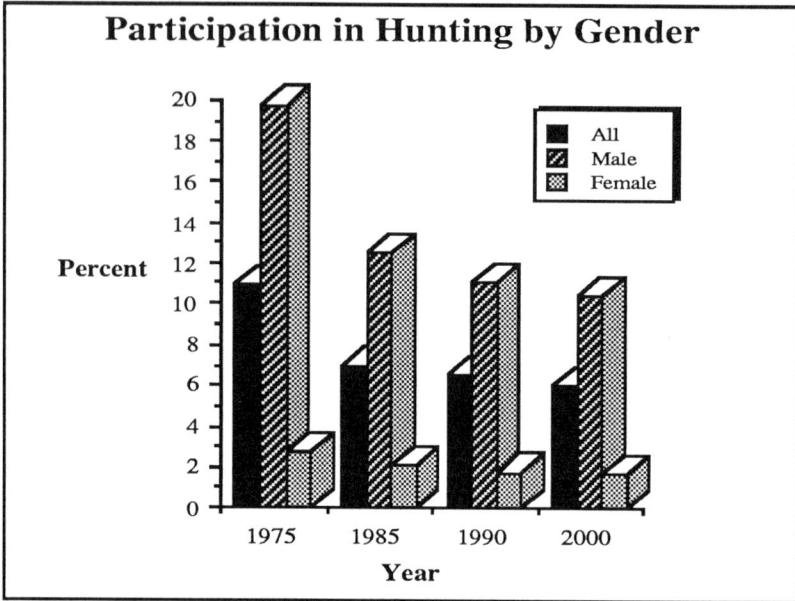

For 1985, the SMS data on frequency indicate that hunting is a regular activity for relatively few. Less than 3 percent of the adult population went hunting as often as once a month. Hunting, then, tends to be a "special event" activity for a predominately male set of participants.

Cohort analysis

Hunting is not an activity restricted to the young. Rates remain fairly stable up to the age of 60 according to the NRS data, and they decline only gradually for those between 45 and 64 years according to the SMS surveys. The shift is among younger males whose participation seems to have declined about 30 percent from 1979 to 1985. As that cohort moves through the life course, they are not likely to increase their hunting rates. Further, when they are the teaching and nurturing generation, they will compound the loss as they are less likely to introduce their children to the activity.

Participation in Hunting by Age

Age	Percentage
65+	2.8
55-64	4.4
45-54	5.5
35-44	8.1
25-34	9.3
18-24	9.6

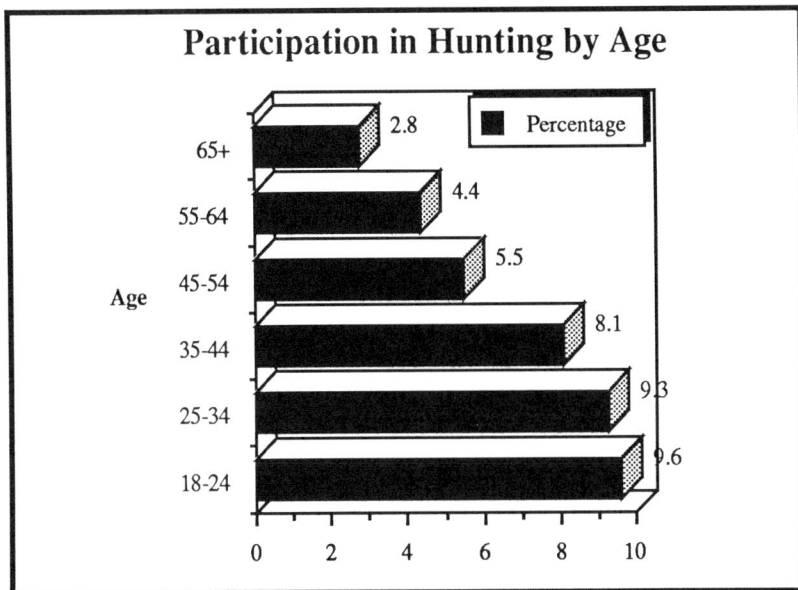

Target markets

Hunters have tended to come disproportionately from areas with access to game environments. With increased urbanization, that group of regular hunters has been reduced and has not been fully replaced by city-dwelling hunters taking special trips to hunting locales.

On the other hand, hunters are distributed rather evenly across the demographic categories.

The major loss in participation will likely occur among the urban Discretionaries who have come from more rural and Middle

Participation by Education Level

Education level	% hunting
Less than HS grad	5.7
High school grad	8.0
Some college	7.5
College graduate	6.2

mass family backgrounds. The data, however, give no clear picture of the trend.

Participation by Income Levels	
Income level	% hunting
-$10,000	4.6
$10 to 24,999	7.7
$25 to 34,999	7.4
$35 to 49,999	7.0
$50,000+	6.5

Future projections

The number of women who hunt decreased slightly from 2.7 percent to 2.1 percent from 1976 to 1985. There are still about six male hunters for every female, however. The cohort of males who are hunting less indicates future long-term declines in hunting participation. Especially with the father-son socialization pattern, every reduction for those cohorts entering childrearing periods will be compounded in the future. That change along with increase urbanization suggests a gradual but significant reduction in hunting for the remainder of the century.

RECREATION TARGET MARKETS: HUNTING

G = GROWTH MARKET   P = POTENTIAL MARKET
E = ESTABLISHED MARKET   L = LOW-PROBABILITY MARKET

Category	Low-end	Middle Mass	Discretionaries	High-end
Preparation	L	E	E	L
Free singles	L	E	E	L
Young parents	?	E	L	L
Established	?	E	E	E
Transitionals	L	E	E	E
Late singles	L	E	E	E
Preretirement	L	E	E	E
Active oldsters	L	E	E	E
The frail	L	L	L	L

SAILING

Sailing includes every size of craft from ten-foot dinghies to luxurious yachts powered by engine as well as sail. While the most common form of sailing is "day sailing" with boats that can be transported on trailers and stored in the garage or back yard, cruising on larger bodies of water is also part of the entire spectrum. There is also a complex network of competition sailing with local, national, and international regattas for the various classes of boats. Again, our data do not distinguish the styles of sailing, the bodies of water, or the sophistication of equipment that differentiate the markets.

Long-term trends

Sailing increased dramatically in participation during the 1960s and 1970s. NRS indicates an increase for males from 3 percent to 7 percent and for females from 2 percent to 5 percent between 1965 and 1983. The Nielsen survey reports increases in sailors of 4 percent from 1973 to 1976, 19 percent from 1976 to 1979, and 23 percent from 1979 to 1982. The greatest increases seem to be in the college-educated and higher-income adults, but they are consistent across age categories.

Short-term trends

The short-term gains are less dramatic, suggesting a possible slight decline or at most some growth at a decreasing rate. Increases may be continuing for women, but not for men over age 35. At present, sailboarding appears to be the growth water-and-sail activity for males under age 25.

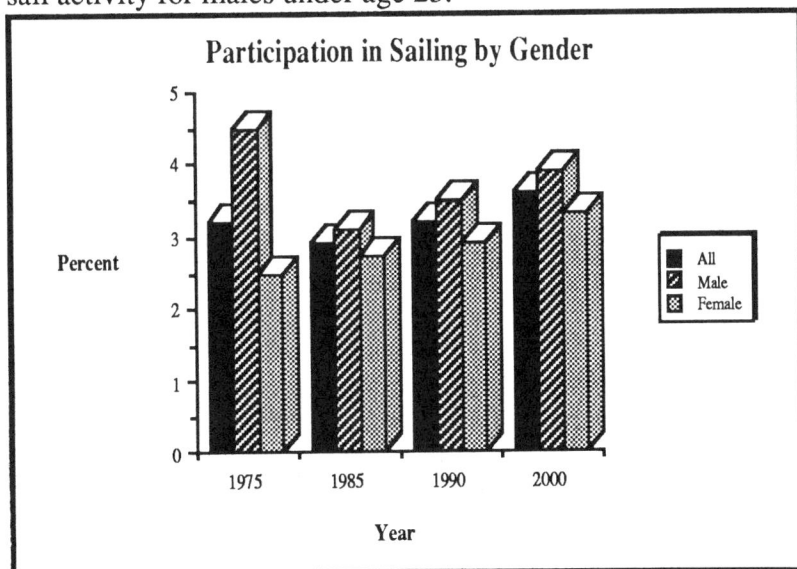

Participation in Sailing by Gender

Frequency of participation in sailing suggests that it is an occasional event for most. In the MRI survey, over 80 percent of the 3.4 percent of the adult population who sailed at all did so ten days or less. The SMS data are consistent, showing that over 70 percent went sailing less than ten times. Again, the 20-80 rule applies with 20 percent of those who sail providing 80 percent of the participation and markets.

Cohort analysis

Sailing is not an activity just for the young, and styles of sailing may vary through the life course. Young sailors are most likely to compete in "wet sailing" single-handers and now on sailboards. Family sailors often use boats large enough to carry 4 to 6 persons for the day or even longer. Cruising is the style for those who can afford the larger boats, usually younger adults without children and those in the pre-retirement period.

The age breakdown is remarkably firm up to retirement age. Decreases in sailing for those over age 35 are about 20 percent for each ten years. The 25- to 34-year-old-cohort has demonstrated the greatest stability and suggests the possibility of persistence through the life course. Also, the "boomer" cohort maintains a relatively high level of participation, over 4 percent.

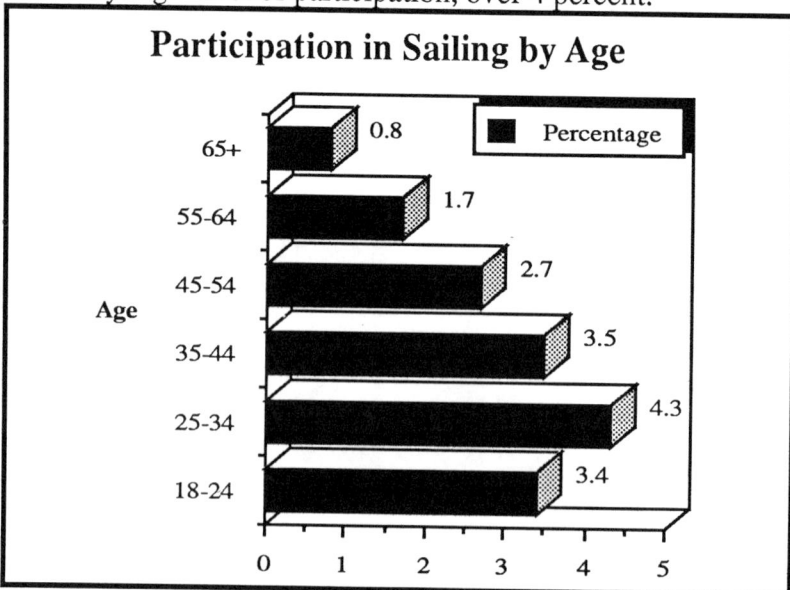

Participation in Sailing by Age

Target markets

Sailing is clearly an upscale recreation activity. It is strongly related to both education levels and income.

Participation by Education Level	
Education level	% sailing
Less than HS grad	1.8
High school grad	1.8
Some college	4.4
College graduate	7.2

Participation by Income Level	
Income level	% sailing
-$10,000	1.8
$10 to 24,999	2.8
$25 to 34,999	5.2
$35 to 49,999	5.7
$50,000+	7.0

The key target markets are the younger Discretionaries and High-enders who have not turned their recreation to-ward the nurture of young children. They generally prefer styles of sailing that maximize excitement, speed over the water, and skill-development. The same economic groups re-emerge as target markets as their children become old enough to be safe on the boats. Many will then move to day sailing and cruising styles. Markets for sailboats larger than 25 feet or so remain primarily among those at the high-income economic levels. The size of boats and related styles are highly correlated with income. Overnight cruising is largely an elite activity.

Future projections

Sailing may not experience the same dramatic rate of increase that characterized the 1960s and 1970s, but it should have gradual growth, especially since young adults are the growth cohort. Also, the large "boomer" cohort has been at least stable in participation rates. The longer-term projections for sailing are closely related to the state of the economy and distribution of incomes. An increase of upper-income Discretionaries in the cohorts now in their 20s and 30s will produce consistent growth in sailing participation. Styles of sailing will vary according to period in the life course as

RECREATION TARGET MARKETS: SAILING

G = GROWTH MARKET   P = POTENTIAL MARKET
E = ESTABLISHED MARKET   L = LOW-PROBABILITY MARKET

Category	Low-end	Middle Mass	Discretionaries	High-end
Preparation	L	P	G	G
Free singles	L	P	G	G
Young parents	L	L	P	P
Established	L	L	G	E
Transitionals	L	L	G	P
Late singles	L	P	G	P
Preretirement	L	L	G	G
Active oldsters	L	L	P	P
The frail	L	L	L	L

well as by income. One factor limiting growth is the current shortage of marina space for mooring and docking boats. Such space is costly and limited near cities. Unless this shortage is alleviated, the sailing styles most likely to increase are those in which boats can be brought to the water rather than stored there. Another problematic factor is the current increase in board sailing among water enthusiasts aged 25 and under. The extent to which they switch to sailboats as they age may figure in the development of future demand.

CROSS-COUNTRY SKIING

Cross-country or "Nordic" skiing is a relatively recent entry into the recognized spectrum of resource-based recreation activities. As a consequence, we have no long-term trend data available. Further, of all the outdoor activities with participation rates greater than 1 percent, it is the most limited in range of participation. Nordic skiers are not only limIted to winter climates, but to specified market segments.

The long-term trend through the 1970s was clearly one of consistent, moderate growth. The activity that was hardly known in the United States before 1965 claimed a larger and larger number of adult participants. Although reliable figures are not available, Nordic skiing grew from a very small base in 1965 to its current level. Promotion efforts helped spur the growth, and skiers themselves recognized its value for winter physical conditioning and the opportunity to avoid the long lines at ski lifts. For many participants who do not live near mountains, Nordic skiing is also an accessible alternative to the time and travel costs of downhill skiing.

While frequency is variable due to weather and the availability of snow, the frequency patterns for Nordic skiing are similar to

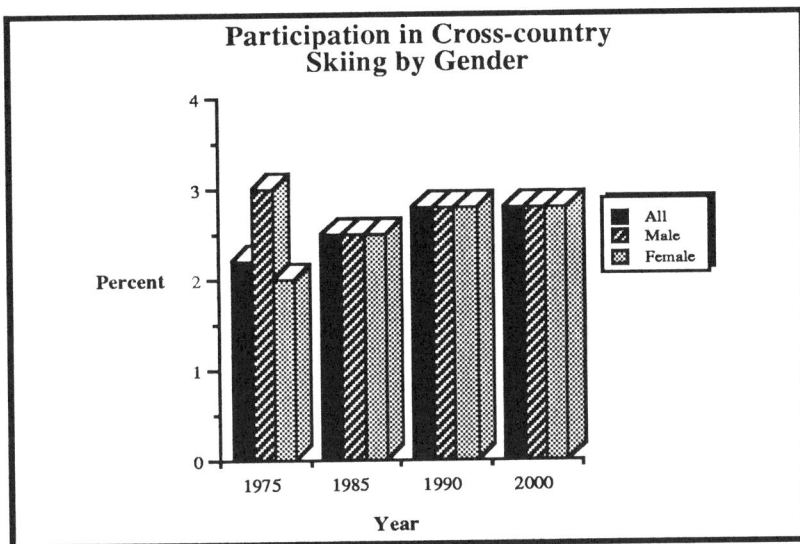

Participation in Cross-country Skiing by Gender

other outdoor activities. Both the MRI and SMS data indicate that 80 percent of participants ski fewer than ten times a year. About 10 percent combined access to snow and commitment levels that have them on skis twenty or more times during the season. Much of the leveling or reduction in participation was among those who were very occasional skiers.

Short-term trends

A peak seems to have been reached in cross-country skiing participation in the early 1980s. Limitations on snow conditions, variations from winter to winter, physical requirements, and the need to be outdoors in the cold all may have been factors in reaching the participation plateau. Further, interest in Nordic

Participaton by Education Level

Education level	% Nordic Skiing
Less than HS grad	.6
High school graduate	1.6
Some college	3.8
College graduate	5.5

skiing has been limited to participants with higher levels of education. Whatever the factors, the shorter-term trend indicates that the growth rate has leveled.

Participation by Income Level

Income level	% sailing
-$10,000	.7
$10 to 24,999	1.8
$25 to 34,999	4.1
$35 to 49,999	4.6
$50,000+	5.4

Cohort analysis

Nordic skiing shows little age-differentiation up to age 50 or so. And unlike so many recreation activities requiring some physical skill and exertion, the youngest cohort has never led in participation. Nordic skiing attracts those past the Preparation period in the life course. This means that continued participation by educated "boomers" offers a possibility for moderate growth in the next few years. The key is probably the extent to which such skiing becomes a "family activity" in the repertoire of Establishment members of the "boomer" cohort.

Target markets

Demand for Nordic skiing has been concentrated disproportionately among those with higher levels of education. Introduction to new participants is even concentrated among those with education at graduate and professional schools. It is an "elite" activity, not by income level as much as in factors related to education and culture.

RECREATION TARGET MARKETS: CROSS-COUNTRY SKIING

G = GROWTH MARKET   P = POTENTIAL MARKET
E = ESTABLISHED MARKET   L = LOW-PROBABILITY MARKET

Category	Low-end	Middle Mass	Discretionaries	High-end
Preparation	L	L	E	E
Free singles	L	P	G	P
Young parents	L	P	G	P
Established	L	P	G	P
Transitionals	L	L	P	?
Late singles	L	L	P	?
Preretirement	L	P	G	P
Active oldsters	L	L	P	P
The frail	L	L	L	L

The evident target market is men and women aged 25 to 55 who have high levels of education. The sport is not costly, so income requirements are only those of the moderate equipment costs. It is, however, an activity into which new participants are introduced more by those in their social groups than by market promotion. One important trend is that there is now no gender difference in participation. It is an activity equally suited for men and women and in which they can participate together.

DOWNHILL SKIING

Downhill skiing is a very cost-intensive activity. Equipment is expensive, and new technologies call for frequent replacement. Downhill skiing is a travel-based event for many participants. They have to set aside a block of time to get to the resource. Once there, they are usually in a high-cost economic and social environment. As a consequence, Alpine skiing is a highly income-differentiated activity. While it has been primarily an activity for the young, recent trends suggest that the age-concentration may be lessening with more skiers over age 35.

Long-term trends

Alpine skiing has demonstrated considerable growth since 1965. This increase in participation is reflected in dramatic growth in businesses that provide equipment, facilities,and related lodging and other services. NRS shows an increase of from 5 percent to 10 percent for males and 3 percent to 7 percent for females from 1965 to 1983. The Nielsen surveys report great increases in the number of downhill skiers: 42 percent from 1973 to 1976, 40 percent from 1976 to 1979, and 27 percent from 1979 to 1982. This increase is more dramatic because Nordic and Alpine skiing were combined in the 1965 NRS figures.

Short-term trends

Short-term trends are confounded by weather variations from one season to another. Lack of snow and early thaws can reduce the number of skiers dramatically in a year. Nevertheless, the short-term trends do suggest a leveling of participation, especially among males aged 18 to 24.

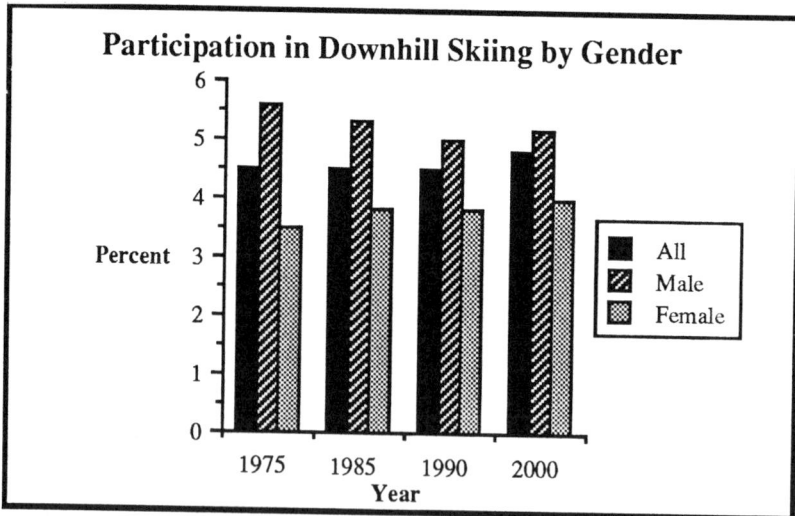

Participation in Downhill Skiing by Gender

The rates are so different between the NRS and Simmons surveys that it is difficult to estimate how the long- and short-term trends articulate. In general, however, indications show market saturation with some question raised about the number of new entrants in the Preparation period of the life course.

Skiing frequency is limited to the resource requirement of snow-packed runs in steep terrain. Snow-making and even artificial hills cannot fully replace the appeal of the New England and Western mountains and even of the European Alps. It is no surprise, then, that the 20-80 rule operates so powerfully. Probably fewer than 20 percent of skiers are on the slopes more than ten days during the season. The SMS survey indicates that less than ten percent ski as often as 25 days a year. This figure, however, does not represent the importance of a one-week trip to those who plan one each year.

Cohort analysis

Those who began skiing during the boom period of the 1960s and 1970s seem to remain committed to the activity. By 1984, the 35- to 44-year-old age category had increased 30 percent from 1980. At the same time, the entry cohort aged 18 to 24 dropped off over 20 percent. This lower rate of entry was almost entirely among males since female participation actually increased slightly.

The stronger cohorts for downhill skiing appear to be the "boomers" and those in the cohort ahead of them. The rates at which current teens and early 20s-age people will take up this cost-intensive activity may depend on their success in the labor market as well as the development of relatively inexpensive

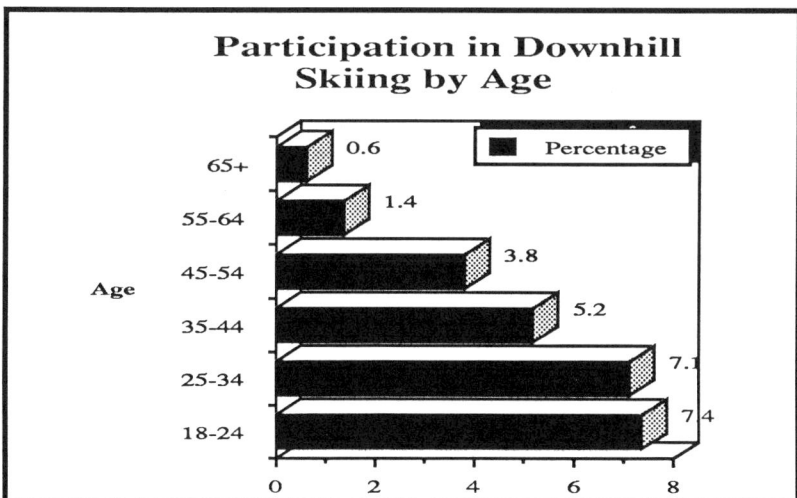

Participation in Downhill Skiing by Age

Age	Percentage
65+	0.6
55-64	1.4
45-54	3.8
35-44	5.2
25-34	7.1
18-24	7.4

opportunities. If Alpine skiing continues to develop as an upscale activity with elaborate facilities and high costs, then its markets may be limited by economic factors more than interest or age-related abilities.

Target markets

Income remains the primary differentiating factor in Alpine skiing. Even the age range of participation, generally from youth through age 45, is less limiting than costs. Discretionaries and those with the highest incomes are clearly the major market for Alpine skiing. Some ski on a careful budget or find low-cost environments, but they are the exception. For most, skiing is just not seriously considered by those not prepared to spend money. The greatest likelihood for expansion would seem to be those in the middle age categories who want to continue or even increase their skiing and who can afford to do so.

RECREATION TARGET MARKETS: DOWNHILL SKIING

G = GROWTH MARKET   P = POTENTIAL MARKET
E = ESTABLISHED MARKET   L = LOW-PROBABILITY MARKET

Category	Low-end	Middle Mass	Discretionaries	High-end
Preparation	L	L	P	E
Free singles	L	L	G	G
Young parents	L	L	P	E
Established	L	L	G	G
Transitionals	L	L	G	G
Late singles	L	L	G	G
Preretirement	L	L	G	G
Active oldsters	L	L	P	P
The frail	L	L	L	L

Future projections

The future of downhill skiing participation depends, of course, on two factors. The first is the state of the economy and the numbers in the younger cohorts with adequate discretionary incomes. The second is the development of opportunities and their relative costs. To break out of the current economic limitations, ski slopes will have to become accessible to moderate-income, younger people; equipment and instruction must become more affordable. Economic rather than demographic factors are pivotal for such a cost-intensive activity. A wider supply of opportunities may, however, aid in creating demand.

OTHER RESOURCE-BASED RECREATION ACTIVITIES

A number of other outdoor recreation activities show even less complete trend data on participation. In the following activities summaries, we will provide briefer analyses of participation.

BIRDWATCHING

Birdwatching is often coupled with "nature study" as a type of activity. The long-term trend is one of increased participation. The National Recreation surveys report that participation doubled from 1965 to 1983.

Participation in Bird Watching		
Age	1965	1983
12 to 24	5	10
25 to 39	5	12
40 to 59	6	12
60+	5	13
Education		
Never finished high school		6
High school graduate		13
College graduate		17
Gender		
Male	5	11
Female	6	12

The 1984 SMS survey, as usual, shows somewhat smaller percentages of participation with a total of 4.6 percent, of whom 59 percent were females. Other factors in the SMS survey are similar.

The most remarkable market segmentation dimension is that participation continues through the adult life course and into early

78

Participation by Age	
Age	Percentage
18 to 24	1.9
25 to 34	3.2
35 to 44	6.6
45 to 54	6.6
55 to 64	6.7
65	6.4

Education	Percentage
Less than high school graduate	3.6
High school graduate	4.6
Some college	4.5
College graduate	6.4

retirement. The long-term increase would seem to be based on the higher education levels of each cohort entering the group aged 40 and older. The established demand is from the college-educated at all adult age levels. This trend should be reinforced as organizations such as the Audubon Society organize and promote such activity. Also, greater interest may be developed through special television programming on nature subjects. Education, then, will continue to be the major distinguishing factor in participation in birdwatching and other nature study.

Frequency of participation (SMS) indicates that of the 4.6 percent who engage in birdwatching, 58 percent did so ten days or less, 18 percent did so for 11 to 41 days, and 23 percent for 42 days or more. Again, about 20 percent did their birdwatching about once a week or more often.

CANOEING AND KAYAKING

Current marketing data are not available for this activity, which is clearly increasing in participation. NRS data support a long-term growth in participation.

Participation in Canoeing and Kayaking by Age and Gender

Age	1965	1983
12 to 24	8	14
25 to 39	3	9
40 to 59	2	6
60+	..	1
Gender		
Males	4	10
Females	3	7

Education	1983
Never finished high school	1
High school graduate	7
College graduate	13
Income	
-$5,000	6
$5 to 14,999	5
$15 to 24,999	8
$25 to 49,999	12
$50,000+	10

Canoeing is a growth activity, and participation is based on access to rivers as well as back country. The established markets are among youth and young adults, with the most specific target being upper-education and income students and young singles. Markets seem to be developing among older adults in their 40s and 50s. These would be concentrated primarily among the Discretionaries with at least some college education.

Some technological developments in more portable and safe equipment may also enhance participation. Uncertain growth would be among Middle mass markets, especially those in Establishment periods. On the negative side, the saturation of resources and crowding in some areas may inhibit canoeing and kayaking.

In general, this is an activity with increased participation across the adult life span. Fiberglass crafts have made such boating less expensive and more convenient. Rivers have become recognized as attractive recreation environments. Crowding is a problem in some areas, but the participation base appears varied enough to sustain further growth. The key target markets may be mixed-sex singles groups and families with older children seeking outdoor recreation that is interesting and challenging for the entire family.

HORSEBACK RIDING

Riding horses underwent a major participation shift when the horse was replaced as the primary mode of private transportation. Now riding is almost entirely recreational except for special uses on ranches.

Long-term trends

The long-term trend seems to be one of reduced participation. The drop from 1965 to 1983 was from 16 percent to 8 percent for males and from 17 percent to 10 percent for females. The reduction was primarily among those in the younger age category: 24 percent to 18 percent for those aged 18 to 24. The drop was less than 10 percent for those aged 25 to 39 and about 5 percent for those aged 40 to 59. This trend suggests that younger cohorts are less likely to ride as they move through the life course.

Short-term trends

The data indicate that the short-term trend is also downward: The gradual downward trend is consistent across education and income levels. It would appear that the cohort of women now in their 50s has maintained a higher level of participation than those younger or older. They are not being replaced at the same level, however, by those now in their 20s, 30s, and 40s. A number of teens still ride. They are more often female than male and usually from middle or upper income families. The size of that cohort would appear to be shrinking, probably due to urbanization and the costs of outdoor space. Of those who rode, 85 percent did

Participation in Horseback Riding by Age and Gender			
Age	1979	1982	1985
18 to 24	11.7	10.0	6.7
25 to 34	6.7	6.0	5.3
35 to 44	.4	4.8	3.7
45 to 54	2.3	3.3	3.3
55 to 64	0.8	2.3	1.1
65+	0.9	0.8	0.6
Gender			
Male	4.5	4.6	3.8
Female	5.3	5.0	4.5

so fewer than ten days. Just over 10 percent rode as often as once a week.

Target markets

The different styles of horseback riding are concealed by the aggregate figures. One group is of moderate income and is more rural in geographical location. Another of quite high income is engaged in specialized kinds of riding in up-scale suburban areas. A third style is that of the occasional rider, usually young, who can't afford to do more than rent by the hour. To reverse the decline in participation, this rental group would have to gain in discretionary income and make a central commitment to the activity.

Future projections

The future, then, gives no clear suggestion that the trend of gradually declining participation will be reversed. The costs of space as well as horse boarding and care are not likely to fall. As a result, horseback riding will continue to be an activity for a small number who are highly committed, youth in rural locales, and the high-end specialists with their elite styles of participation.

SNOWMOBILING

Market studies have divided snowmobiling markets into two types: farmers and others in rural areas who use the vehicles in their work and the recreational market. The rural-use market has been stable. The recreational market, however, has declined since about 1975.

Long-term trends

The recreational aspects of snowmobiling developed as the vehicle was developed and marketed in the 1960s and early 1970s. Unfortunately, participation data are available only for the period in which the cycle peaked and began to decline. The Nielsen survey indicates a 19 percent increase in snowmobiling from 1973 to 1976 followed by a 6 percent decline from 1976 to 1979 and stability from 1979 to 1982. The long-term trend follows the product life cycle: rapid growth from 1965 to about 1975 followed by a decline and plateauing in the following five years.

Short-term trends

A reliable trend analysis cannot be developed from only three data points, especially for an activity that is affected by local and regional weather conditions. The SMS data, however, do suggest that the stability of the early 1980s may be consistent with weather conditions.

Short-term Participation in Snowmobiling

Age	1979	1982	1985
18 to 24	4.7	3.3	4.1
25 to 34	2.9	2.4	3.2
35 to 44	3.5	2.0	2.4
45 to 54	2.1	1.7	2.1
55 to 64	.8	1.1	1.8
65+	.4	.1	.5
Gender			
Male	2.8	2.2	3.2
Female	2.3	1.5	1.6

Snowmobiling is, as expected, predominately a Middle mass activity with a bias toward rural male participation. The greatest decline in participation is among those under age 25, a trend that does not offer high hope for a reversal of the downward trend.

Factors in the decline include safety concerns, inconsistent snow conditions in many areas, and market saturation with subsequent decline from the peak period. The growth period was

Participation in Snowmobiling According to Education

Education level	1982	1984	1985
Less than high school grad	1.2	1.1	.9
High school graduate	3.6	2.5	3.5
Some College	2.8	2.9	2.5
College graduate	1.7	1.3	2.4

rapid as the new vehicle was introduced and promoted, but inherent limitations caused the peak to be reached in a few years.

Target markets

The main markets remain rural and Middle mass adults, rural "users" and Middle mass "recreation snowmobilers." Frequency of use data suggest that about 75 percent of snowmobilers used their machines less than ten days in 1985. That figure may reflect weather problems as much as interest. Nevertheless, such low usage rates do not bode well for the replacement market in the future. Projections seem to depend on the extent to which recreational riders will introduce friends and family to the activity. The markets might be expanded as a family and "environmental" activity, but failing that, only excitement-oriented Middle mass males are likely to supplement the rural use markets.

WATER-SKIING

Water-skiing is an activity differentiated by both age and income. It requires high levels of physical competence, a boat powerful enough to pull the skier, and bodies of water large enough to accommodate the activity.

Long-term trends

Water-skiing has been a growth activity in the past decades. NRS reports an increase from 1965 to 1983 of 8 percent to 11 percent for males and 5 percent to 7 percent for females. By age the increase is disproportionately among the 25- to 39-year-old group, from 5 percent to 12 percent. The increase in participation was 15 percent to 17 percent for those aged 12 to 24 and 1 percent to 4 percent for those aged 40 to 59. Many who began water-skiing as youth seem to be continuing in their young and middle adult periods.

The Nielsen surveys are consistent with the NRS. They indicate increases in participation of 5 percent from 1973 to 1976, 15 percent from 1976 to 1979, and 7 percent from 1979 to 1982.

Water-skiing participation, then, has demonstrated consistent long-term growth.

Short-term trends

More current trends from the SMS indicate that the longer-term trend may be relatively stable.

Short-term Participation in Water-skiing				
Age	1976	1979	1982	1985
18 to 24		14.2	11.5	8.4
25 to 34		6.9	7.3	7.5
35 to 44		5.4	3.7	5.3
45 to 54		2.1	2.1	2.6
55 to 64		1.2	1.1	1.5
65+		0.9	1.0	0.5
Gender				
Male	7.1	7.5	6.3	6.0
Female	2.9	3.9	3.7	3.7
Total	4.9	5.6	4.9	4.8

Female participation may have increased in the 1970s but appears to have stabilized. The only clearly identified trend seems to be a leveling of the former rate of increase.

Target markets

The age of water-skiing participants reflects differences in education levels: 1.8 percent for those not completing high school, 4.8 percent for high school graduates, 8.0 percent for those with some college, and 6.5 percent for those with college degrees. Most participants are concentrated in the student and young adult population from upper-middle to upper-income households. The greatest increase in participation occurs at an income level of $35,000 per year.

Frequency may reflect summer schedules as well as access to water and the necessary equipment. Almost 90 percent of those who water-skied did so ten times or less. Only a tiny fraction of the participants lived in climates and had access to water-skiing so they could engage in the activity as often as once a week. For most it is a special occasion, often related to a vacation or weekend trip.

Water-skiing participation may extend more into young adult and even establishment periods for many of those Discretionaries and High-end adults who began the activity in their youth. Extending the age range would seem more likely than decreasing the costs. Any growth in this stable activity will be among Discretionaries in their 30s and 40s. The potential markets are limited by seasonal problems and access to water for most of the population, coupled with the costs of a tow boat. It is a solid activity, but one with limited growth potential.

SUMMARY: RESOURCE BASED OUTDOOR RECREATION TRENDS

In general, the earlier expansion in outdoor recreation participation seems to have leveled. Rates of participation are decreasing for activities with a rural population base. For those with primary markets among young and mid-life adults with discretionary incomes and college education, the issue is more than one of resources. Where the resources are saturated, participation is not likely to increase. Time as much as money places distance limits on recreation trips. Therefore, increased participation will require greater access to attractive resources. For those in metropolitan areas in the Northeast, such resource gains are unlikely. Even in the West, crowded resources and traffic jams on weekends limit potential increases in resource-based outdoor recreation.

All outdoor recreation, however, does not require trips to special resources such as forests, lakes, seashores, deserts, and mountains. Metropolitan areas also include potential resources for many kinds of water and land activities. Some of the activities analyzed in this chapter, for example, sailing, hiking, waterskiing, cross-country skiing, and fishing, are possible near residences in many areas. Increasingly, markets will respond to public provisions for such activity in and near cities.

COMMUNITY
RECREATION

CHAPTER 4

In some cases, the distinction between resource-based recreation and community-based activities is blurred. Except for those with exceptionally advantageous locations, the resource-based activities generally require traveling to a special environment. A few people may be able to sail from their backyard docks or ski in the adjacent forest, but they are exceptions. The activities included in this chapter are those usually possible in urban neighborhoods. The providers are generally community public recreation agencies or recreation businesses. In cases such as bicycling, no special resources are necessary, although bike paths and trails are desirable.

BICYCLING

Most bicycling is done by children and youth who are trying to get somewhere. Since gas prices increased, more adults have used bikes to get to and from work. As a consequence, purely recreational bicycling cannot be separated from transportation or from trips that combine specific aims with exercise and just being outdoors. It is a "mixed" activity. Nevertheless, some increased participation is recreational as the activity combines a number of desirable elements: group interaction with family and friends, outdoor locales, self-paced physical exertion, and self-selected timetables when the weather permits.

Long-term trends

The National Recreation Surveys show considerable increase in bicycling from 1963 to 1983: from 16 percent to 33 percent for males and from 17 percent to 32 percent for females. The greatest increase is for adults.

88

The Nielsen surveys, on the other hand, are less clear-cut. They show an increase of 12 percent from 1973 to 1976, a loss of 7 percent from 1976 to 1979, and a small gain of 3 percent from 1979 to 1982. Since those figures are consistent with the SMS

Participation in Bicycling by Age		
Age	1965	1983
12 to 24	48	55
25 to 39	20	37
40 to 59	12	22
60+	1	7

statistics for the same period, the growth in participation spurred by the gas crisis of the 1970s appears to have dwindled.

Short-term trends

The SMS surveys also indicate a decline during the period 1976 to 1979 as people adjusted to higher gas prices and shortages were alleviated. Bicycling again became a recreational activity rather than an energy-saving substitute for motor transportation. The long-term increase in biking by adults up to the age of 45 or even 60 seems to have continued, however.

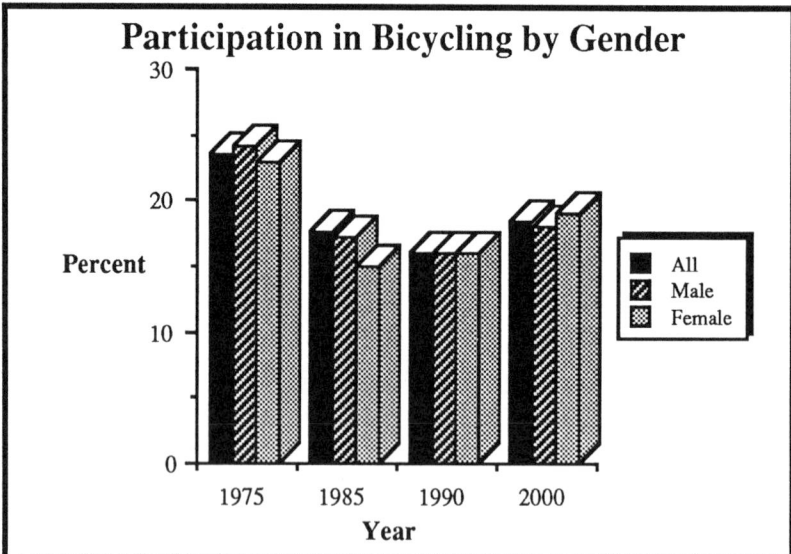

Participation in Bicycling by Gender

Frequency of participation figures gives some idea of commitment to bicycling. The MRI data indicate that 55 percent of those who rode bicycles did so ten days a year or less and 18 percent did so as often as once a week. The SMS data indicate a somewhat more varied pattern with about 40 percent riding bikes ten days or less, 45 percent riding between 11 and 59 days, and 15 percent riding 60 days or more a year. Both indicate that most adults ride occasionally rather than regularly and for recreation rather than for transportation.

Cohort Analysis

The "boomer" cohort is critical because of its size and the fact that their participation rates have not fallen compared to those under age 35. The likelihood that bicycling can maintain its market share for that cohort is the way to longer-term growth. Since crowding and cost are not limitations, no structural factors seem likely to reverse this trend.

Target markets

The composition of bicycling markets has experienced some shifts. Female participation declined less than male participation between 1976 and 1984. The "boomers" increased their rates, suggesting possible market strength for the future.

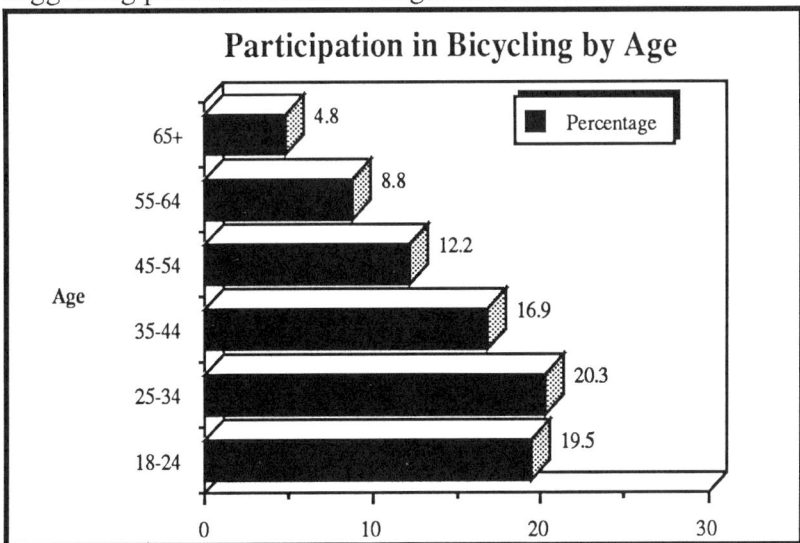

Participation in Bicycling by Age

Age	Percentage
65+	4.8
55-64	8.8
45-54	12.2
35-44	16.9
25-34	20.3
18-24	19.5

Bicycling is not restricted to elites, but it is almost evenly spread across lower-middle to upper categories in both education and income. With its persistence into middle age, bicycling

90

combines a number of satisfaction dimensions, easy access, moderate cost, and on-demand timetables, at least in season.

Participation in Bicycling by Education and Income	
Education	% Bicycling
Less than HS grad	7.5
HS grad	13.5
Some college	20.4
College grad	21.9
Income	
-$10,000	7.7
$10-24,999	14.7
$25-34,999	19.2
$35-49,999	19.6
$50,000+	18.5

With declines occurring only for those aged 45 and older, the potential markets for bicycling are broad: they include Middle mass and Discretionary men and women through Establishment and into Preretirement periods of the life course.

Future projections

The popularity of bicycling in the "baby boom" cohort suggests consistent growth in future participation. Bicycling has been rediscovered as an aerobic, health-enhancing activity by some who have experienced running injuries. It is limited by the concern about accidents in proximity to automotive traffic.

RECREATION TARGET MARKETS: BICYCLING

G = GROWTH MARKET   P = POTENTIAL MARKET
E = ESTABLISHED MARKET   L = LOW-PROBABILITY MARKET

Category	Low-end	Middle Mass	Discretionaries	High-end
Preparation	E	E	E	E
Free singles	L	P	G	P
Young parents	L	G	G	P
Established	L	P	G	L
Transitionals	L	P	P	?
Late singles	L	P	P	E
Preretirement	L	P	P	P
Active oldsters	L	P	P	P
The frail	L	L	L	L

Expansion of dedicated bike trails would probably boost recreational riding. Recreational bicycling tends to be a weekend activity, often organized with friends and family. As such, it combines exercise in outdoor environments without the need for special travel. If safety concerns can be reduced, long-term participation growth can be expected.

BOWLING

Bowling takes place primarily in market-sector facilities. A cycle of decline in the provision of bowling centers has been followed by current efforts to refurbish both facilities and the image of the activity. The bowling industry tries to promote the image of a "sport for all." This is accurate in that participation is distributed up to age 55 and for the Middle mass income and education levels. Also, it is indoors and not subject to weather disturbance. The gender gap is closing so that the bowling center is a place for both men and women to meet. Nevertheless, the decline in participation is significant but gradual.

Long-term trends

The most negative indication is that many bowling centers have been closed. Brunswick alone closed one-third of their 250 centers in the past decade. Participation rates, however, do not show a consistent decline. The Nielsen surveys recorded a 16 percent increase in participation from 1973 to 1976. This gain during the youth of the "boomer" cohort was followed by measured decline: 2 percent from 1976 to 1979 and 7 percent from 1979 to 1982.

Short-term trends

The SMS data report stability in participation rates for both men and women from 1976 to 1979 followed by significant reductions in the early 1980s.

What is significant is that ALL the decline is among the younger age cohorts. Participation among the age category from 18 to 24 went from 35.7 percent in 1979 to 28.1 percent in 1985 and in the 25- to 34-year-old category from 28.8 percent to 23.4 percent. The reduction occurs among those in the lower income

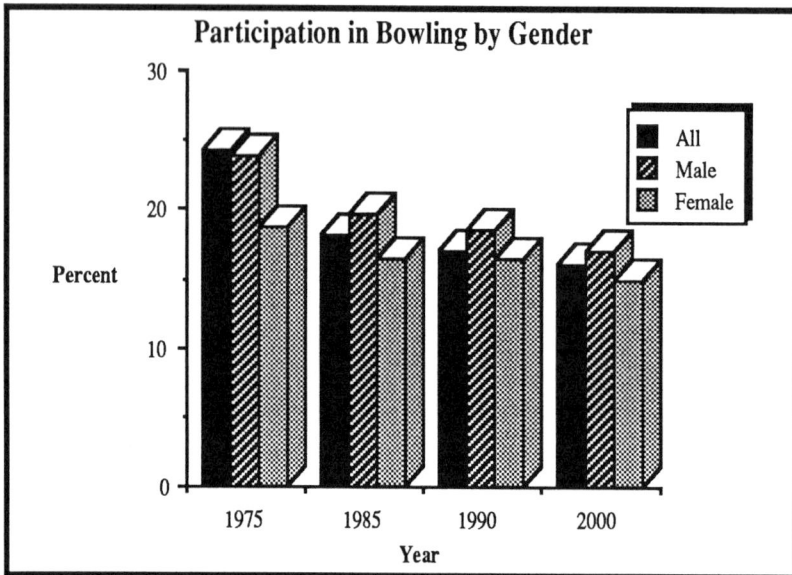

Participation in Bowling by Gender

Percent

Legend:
- All
- Male
- Female

Years: 1975, 1985, 1990, 2000

Year

categories whose household incomes are from $10,000 to $25,000 and to a slightly lower degree among those with higher incomes.

Bowling seems to be divided between "regulars" and "occasionals." Of those who bowled, 60 percent did so ten times or less per year. The faithful cadre of once-a-week bowlers numbered about 10 percent of the total.

Cohort analysis

The "boomer" cohort is now in the age period when maximum participation in bowling would have been expected. Their reduced rates of participation compared to previous cohorts suggest a long-term problem in total numbers of participants. On the other hand, bowling is a sport that has retained a significant number of older participants. Retention is a critical issue as cohorts enter their 50s and 60s.

Target markets

The traditional target market was and continues to be blue-collar men. Bowling is not an elite sport. Women constitute the market segment that has grown in relative importance in the last decade. And, the physical requirements of bowling are such that

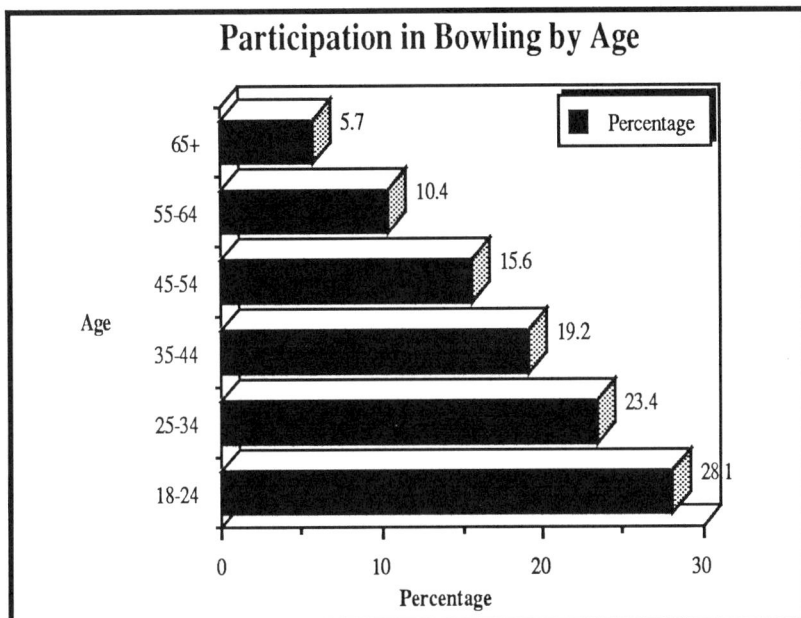

Participation in Bowling by Age

Age	Percentage
65+	5.7
55-64	10.4
45-54	15.6
35-44	19.2
25-34	23.4
18-24	28.1

it can be continued well into Pre-retirement and even into Active oldster periods. The reduction for younger adults is a major concern, so retaining the older groups may be the most viable target markets for providers. Refurbishing centers to compete with other recreation locales may enhance the image of the activity for the under-35 cohorts.

Future projections

Failure to develop interest among the "boomer" cohort is a serious concern for the industry. Unless that trend can be reversed by site improvements and promotion, the long-term future for bowling may be one of continued, gradual decline. Nevertheless, some factors might mitigate this trend: in winter climates, the bowling center can provide an attractive meeting place for both men and women while outdoor activity is limited; and special promotions for the retired may also provide growth markets.

RECREATION TARGET MARKETS: BOWLING			
G = GROWTH MARKET P = POTENTIAL MARKET E = ESTABLISHED MARKET L = LOW-PROBABILITY MARKET			
Category	Low-end	Middle Mass	Discretionaries	High-end
Preparation	L	E	E	E
Free singles	L	E	E	E
Young parents	L	E	E	L
Established	L	E	E	L
Transitionals	L	P	P	L
Late singles	L	P	P	P
Preretirement	L	P	P	L
Active oldsters	L	P	P	L
The frail	L	L	L	L

FITNESS PROGRAMS

No long-term trend data are available on this relatively new activity. Limited data suggest a fundamental division between organized programs in public and market-provided sites and fitness activity that takes place in or around the home. Organized programs have taken a multitude of forms. Some offer a variety of activities such as aerobic dance, exercise, weight training, and even some indoor sports. Others specialize in a single form of exercise. Some attempt to attract a wide spectrum of participants, while others target their markets more narrowly.

The attention given by the media to "health and fitness" activity has tended to exaggerate the extent of regular participation. The pricing policies of many "fitness centers" reveal that they expect high drop-out rates, 80 percent or more for many programs. The motivations for participation are not just health and fitness. For many, the hopes are more cosmetic than health-related. And some programs have emphasized social aspects of participation, making exercise programs meeting places for singles, young mothers, or other groups that enjoy being together. The failure rate of many businesses suggests that in some areas market saturation has occurred.

Whatever the motivations, it is clear that exercise programs have grown rapidly in the last decade to become a major recreation-related activity. What is less clear is the "activity life cycle" of such programs and activity. What is the evidence that "fitness" is still in a growth phase, that it has peaked, or that it is moving into a plateau stage of development?

Short-term trends

Unfortunately, we have only three data points from the SMS market studies. Prior to 1982, such activity was not included in the national surveys, and there are great inconsistencies among different studies. To maintain consistency, we will use only those studies on which we have relied for other activities.

The Simmons surveys distinguish exercise participation in and outside the home. Even the brief period between 1982 and 1985 shows an increase in participation, but 1985 rates return approximately to the 1982 levels.

Percentages of Participation in Exercise Activities

| Category | Outside home | | | At home | | |
	1982	1984	1985	1982	1984	1985
Male	12.0	14.8	13.0	17.6	19.8	18.9
Female	16.8	17.6	16.2	20.0	20.3	19.2
Total	14.6	16.3	14.7	18.9	19.8	18.9

The figures show rapid growth to a peak reached about 1984. The current life cycle of the activity seems to be declining to a yet-undetermined plateau. Total participation is comparable with the high-rate activities. Physical fitness has obviously become a major category of activity in only a few years.

Other figures suggest that the alleged "boom" may be somewhat exaggerated. First, the 1984 MRI survey asked specifically about "health clubs." Rates of participation at such sites were reported to be much lower: the total was 7.7 percent of the adult population with 6.4 percent of the males and 8.9 percent of the females. It is important, therefore, not to equate regular exercise with any single kind of program or facility.

Second, frequency rates are similar to those for other regular activities. In the MRI study, 41 percent went to health clubs ten times or less and only 30 percent went as often as once a week for the year. If participation less frequent than once a week is actually detrimental to health, as some propose, then some of the "boom" may be casual interest rather than real commitment. Frequency rates for those who claim to have engaged in jogging show even less consistency.

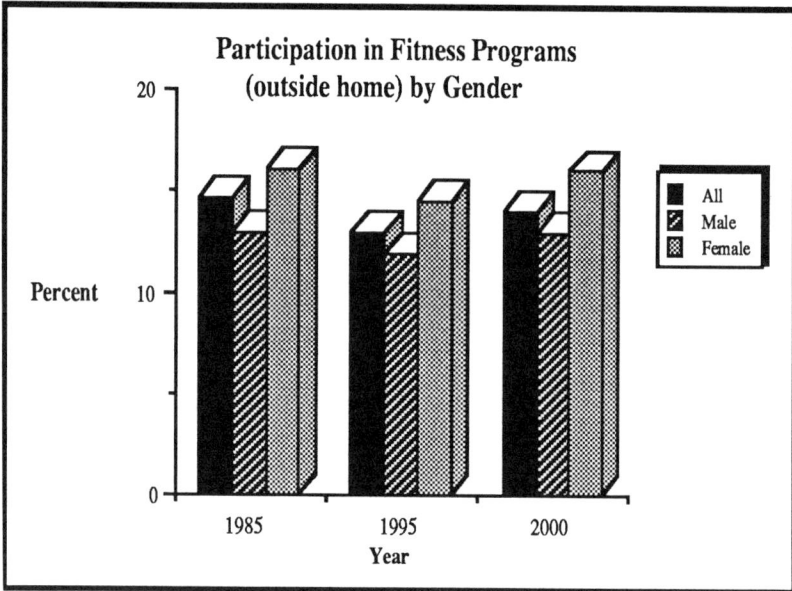

Participation in Fitness Programs (outside home) by Gender

Cohort analysis

As expected, the age distributions for fitness programs is skewed toward the young. Nevertheless, there is significant participation of adults up to retirement age, especially in at-home exercise.

No startling shifts in age distributions occurred between 1982 and 1985. Rates for programs outside the home are consistent up to the age of 55. The cohorts aged 35 to 54 gained most in fitness activity at home, and those under 35 did not increase their at-home exercise. Shifts of only 1 to 3 percent have to be considered unreliable.

Participation in Fitness Programs
(outside home) by Age

Age	Percentage
65+	5
55-64	9.2
45-54	12.2
35-44	17
25-34	20.8
18-24	19.7

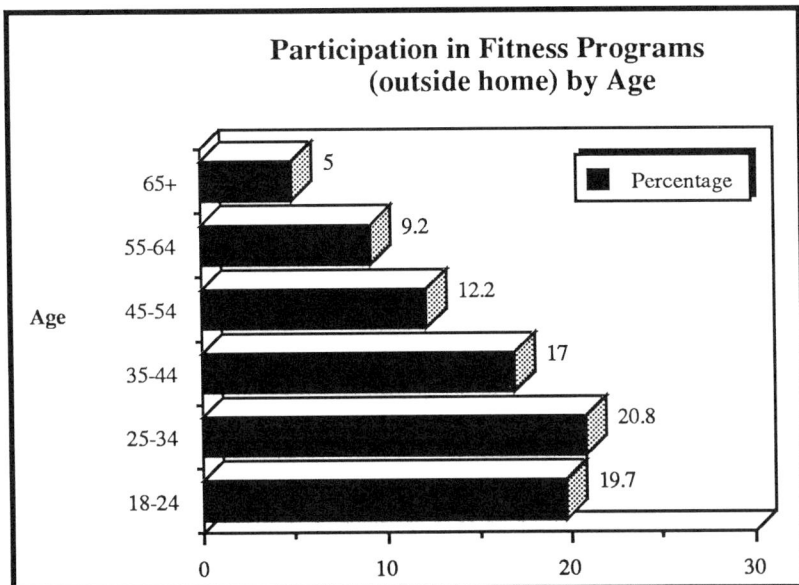

The MRI data show that health clubs are more a phenomenon for young adults than for generic fitness activity. Rates according to age are:

Age 18 to 24 = 12.6 percent
     25 to 34 = 11.0 percent
     35 to 44 = 9.1 percent
     45 to 54 = 5.7 percent
     55 to 64 = 3.4 percent
     65+   = 1.2 percent

The cohorts of greatest interest for future fitness programs are those now in their 20s and 30s. Each older age category shows a marked decline in participation, but it remains over 10 percent up to age 65. Exercise at some locales, however, falls below 10 percent only for those of retirement age. Nevertheless, there are viable markets for programs at every age level. The critical question is continuing commitment. To what extent will the current interest in fitness programs continue among young adults as they move through life course periods when such engagement may become more difficult and demanding?

Target markets

The prime market for fitness programs may be women aged 18 to 34, but no category seems to lack significant participation. Only those with less than high school education and low incomes fall below 10 percent in participation and then only for activity outside the home.

Participation in Fitness Programs by Education and Income		
Education	Outside the home	At home
Less than HS grad	8.0	12.1
HS grad	15.2	19.3
Some college	23.1	26.0
College grad	25.4	28.8
Income		
-$10,000	8.7	12.2
$10-24,999	13.2	19.9
$25-34,999	22.1	23.5
$35-49,999	23.5	24.5
$50,000+	24.4	25.5

Programs outside the home have markedly increased their participation among those with middle or higher incomes who have attended college. Exercise at home is less differentiated by education and income levels than by age. College-educated younger women are the prime market, but not to the exclusion of others in different age and socio-economic categories. It would be useful to know just which programs are attracting different market segments and which have the highest retention rates. But current data show that except for the old and poor, no market segments are excluded from some kind of fitness participation.

RECREATION TARGET MARKETS:
FITNESS PROGRAMS

G = GROWTH MARKET   P = POTENTIAL MARKET
E = ESTABLISHED MARKET   L = LOW-PROBABILITY MARKET

Category	Low-end	Middle Mass	Discretionaries	High-end
Preparation	P	P	G	G
Free singles	P	P	G	G
Young parents	L	L	E	E
Established	L	E	E	E
Transitionals	L	P	G	G
Late singles	L	P	P	P
Preretirement	L	P	G	P
Active oldsters	L	L	P	P
The frail	L	L	L	L

Future projections

Insofar as the development of this kind of activity is based on a new commitment to health and physical fitness, continued rates of participation are likely to cross many categories of the adult population. Because some interests are more cosmetic and constitute a response to marketing promotion and media attention, the life cycle can be expected to peak and decline to a plateau.

Has participation in fitness programs peaked or will the growth continue? Based on current leveling or slight declines, evidence of different levels of commitment, and the general inevitability of the product/activity life cycle, the growth period has likely ended after a peak in about 1984. The decline from that peak should not be overwhelming, although it will close a number of businesses and programs where the market is oversupplied. The decline will hit those programs hardest that require extraordinary effort to get to a special place at a predefined time. A stronger level of participation should continue for on-demand exercise than for narrowly-targetted and expensive programs. Nevertheless, rates of participation through the life course and for both sexes suggest a new level of commitment to exercise. The forms will change as boredom, injuries, costs, inconveniences, and social attachments change. Fitness in some locales, including the home, will likely maintain participation levels as high as 80 percent of peak rates for the remainder of the century. Those planning programs, facilities, and investments should stay ahead of the shifts in forms and types of activity and not become locked into activities popular two years ago.

GOLF

No recreation activity has enjoyed more stable participation or more clearly defined markets than golf. About three times as many men play golf as women. It is disproportionately played by those with discretionary incomes. Almost uniquely, golf participation is consistent across age categories up to age 65 with some continuation through the "Active oldster" period. It is a consistent activity with identifiable markets. Although locales vary with about 45 percent at country clubs or private clubs and 55 percent at municipal or daily fee courses (SMS, 1984), rates of participation have remained quite stable.

Long-term trends

Long-term participation has increased in golf: from 1965 to 1983 male rates increased fom 14 percent to 20 percent and female from 5 percent to 7 percent. The Nielsen surveys show a decline of 3 percent from 1973 to 1976, another small decline of 4 percent from 1976 to 1979, and a gain of 9 percent from 1979 to 1982. The increases reported in the NRS were concentrated more among those aged 40 and above than among the younger cohorts.

An increase in golfing participation in the 1960s appears to have been followed by a peak and slight decline in the 1970s. Now this trend seems to have reversed with gradual participation gains in the later 1970s and early 1980s.

Short-term trends

A small short-term increase in golfing participation is possible in the 1980s. Unlike the increase in the 1960s, the gain is concentrated more among younger golfers under age 45. The decline of the 1970s has been halted and perhaps replaced since

1982 with a slight trend of increasing participation by young adult and establishment men.

Frequency figures suggest that golf is something of a passion for about 10 percent of all players and a very occasional activity for the 50 to 60 percent who play less than ten times a year. About 20 percent played 24 times or more. That could translate into once a week where the season is short and to less frequent golfing in the South and Southwest. Since the frequency rates are not broken down by climate, a rough estimate would be that the 20-80 rule applies: about 20 percent of those who golf at all are the "regulars" on the course at least once a week in season.

Cohort Analysis

Golf is unique among outdoor sports in that it retains older participants. Since it can be somewhat self-paced, golf does not require bursts of strenuous action, and the walking and carrying requirements can be eased by powered carts. Thus older men and women can continue to play through their active middle and later years.

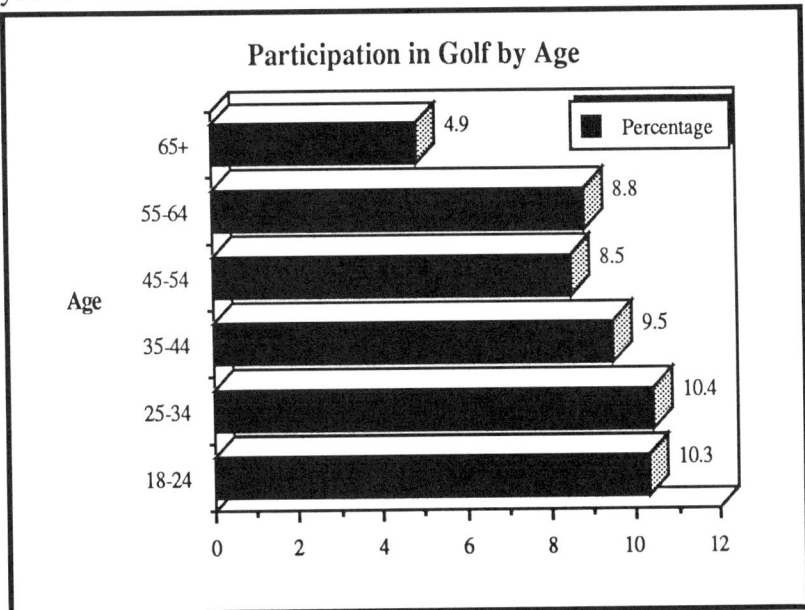

Participation in Golf by Age

Target markets

The consistency of market segments for golf indicates that the markets are well-established. Younger Discretionaries appear to be the only exception as they take time from their careers to pursue a symbol of their preferred lifestyle and status. They would appear to be the most probable growth market, because golfing has been a consistent activity for those in the upper third or so of income and education levels.

The major market for golf continues to be men with discretionary or upper incomes — and their male children — up to the time that physical limitations take their toll. No similar activity is as likely to retain engagement from youth into retirement years.

Participation in Golfing by Education and Income

Education	% Golfing
Less than HS grad	2.9
HS grad	7.9
Some college	13.9
College grad	16.4

Income	
-$10,000	2.5
$10-24,999	6.3
$25-34,999	14.0
$35-49,999	15.4
$50,000+	16.7

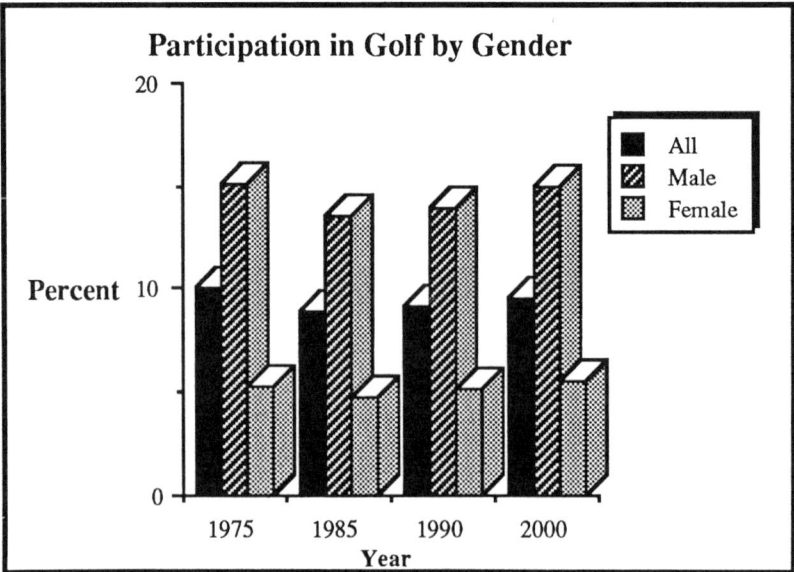

Participation in Golf by Gender

Future projections

Dramatic increases in golfing participation would require two changes: 1) more adults in their 30s and 40s with considerable discretionary income and 2) more accessible golf courses. If the "boomer" cohort does well economically, they could provide more potential golfers. The space-intensive nature of the activity together with the high costs of land in metropolitan areas, however, suggest that the supply of new golf courses will be limited. The recent participation trend of slight increases is likely to continue, but at a very slow rate.

RECREATION TARGET MARKETS: GOLF

G = GROWTH MARKET   P = POTENTIAL MARKET
E = ESTABLISHED MARKET   L = LOW-PROBABILITY MARKET

Category	Low-end	Middle Mass	Discretionaries	High-end
Preparation	L	P	E	E
Free singles	L	P	E	E
Young parents	L	L	P	P
Established	L	L	P	G
Transitionals	L	L	G	G
Late singles	L	L	P	E
Preretirement	L	L	G	E
Active oldsters	L	L	G	E
The frail	L	L	L	L

RACQUETBALL

Racquetball differs from most of the recreation activities in this study because it is new. Data points begin with 1976 and long-term trends are lacking. The new sport expanded rapidly in the 1970s, reached a peak, and then declined to a plateau. The sport became popular so quickly because players could swiftly reach a satisfying level of skill in this short-handle racquet sport. Unlike the longer-handled racquets, the racquetball instrument was designed for an easy introduction to the sport. Moreover, the indoor courts require less space than tennis courts, making it more attractive for winter participation. Easier than squash and more compact than tennis, racquetball zoomed in popularity.

Then something happened. Racquetball peaked by 1978 and entered a period of decline. Some market-sector facilities failed. Others were diversified into "fitness centers," and courts were refitted for aerobics and even volleyball to attract a wider clientele. The transfer from summer tennis to winter racquetball did not quite materialize. Initial enthusiasm waned. Some market areas were saturated. High-cost facilities required high fees. Noontimes and early evenings were filled, but courts were empty for hours each day. Racquetball never really caught on for children, most women, or others outside the upper-income males between the ages of 18 and 40. The activity life cycle has been a classic boom-peak-decline curve. Now the question focuses on the composition of the plateau.

Short-term trends

The Nielsen figures document the boom and peak. Racquetball participation increased 28 percent from 1976 to 1979 and then leveled to a 14 percent increase from 1979 to 1983.

SMS data are available for the periods beginning in 1979. They indicate a slight increase to 1982 followed by a decline in participation in the middle 1980s. Male participation went from 6.7 percent in 1979 to 8.3 percent in 1982 and then to 7.1 percent

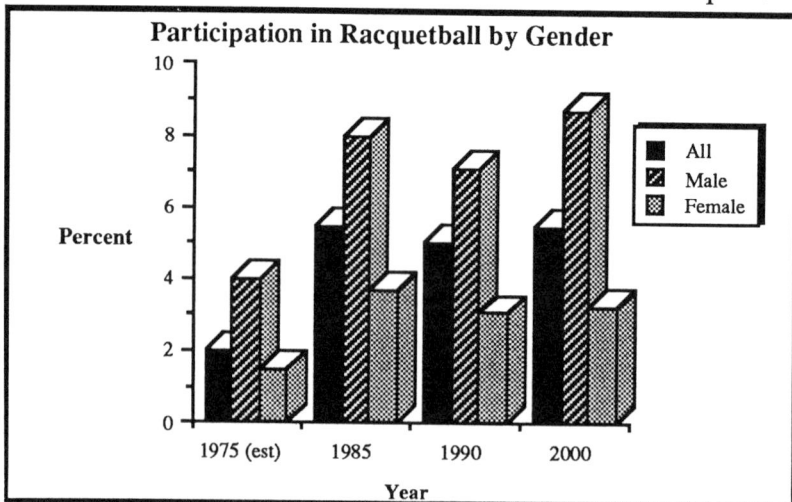

Participation in Racquetball by Gender

in 1985. Female engagement increased from 3.5 percent to 5.0 percent from 1979 to 1982 and then declined back to 3.1 percent in 1985.

NRI and SMS frequency data indicate that over 60 percent of those who played at all did so ten times or less in a year. About 10 percent played once a week or more

Cohort analysis

Racquetball participants are predominately in their 20s and 30s. The percentages of participation are markedly lower for the older cohort. Continuing players will flatten the curve of decline, especially for men in their 40s and 50s. Looking ahead, the major question is the extent to which the decline will be halted and the "boomers" will stay with the sport as they enter their 40s. Currently, considerable participation occurs at colleges and universities and at the special facilities and clubs that cater to younger urban clienteles. Future trends will be determined by the rate at which racquetball retains those who first participated during their years as university students or those who began with a cohort of peers during the growth years of the sport.

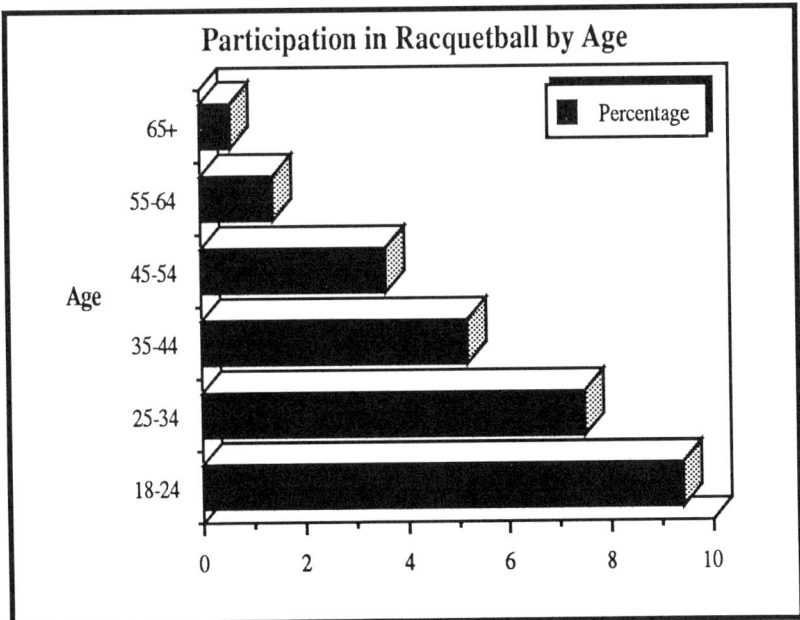

Participation in Racquetball by Age

Target markets

Racquetball is a "specialty" activity. It is limited primarily to young adults with discretionary incomes who have access to facilities in regions with winter climates. The business failures make it unlikely that the market sector will increase in the foreseeable future. The key is the proportion of discretionaries, at least 2:1 male to female, who will stay with the activity and gradually introduce peers to its blend of high-energy exertion in a competitive frame.

Future projections

Limited market segments and opportunities do not indicate any significant growth in participation. Some gain may be realized as "boomers" retain higher rates of participation than those now in their 40s and 50s. That retention, however, will depend on continued access to facilities. Nonprofit organizations may take a larger share of the market unless business providers can solidify markets in areas of relatively high demand. The activity life cycle of racquetball illustrates how market forces can combine with the nature of the activity to gain markets rapidly and then lose them because of age, income, and access-related factors. Costs, schedule, and perhaps lack of transfer from previous

RECREATION TARGET MARKETS: RACQUETBALL

G = GROWTH MARKET   P = POTENTIAL MARKET
E = ESTABLISHED MARKET   L = LOW-PROBABILITY MARKET

Category	Low-end	Middle Mass	Discretionaries	High-end
Preparation	L	L	E	E
Free singles	L	L	E	E
Young parents	L	L	P	P
Established	L	L	P	P
Transitionals	L	L	P	P
Late singles	L	L	L	L
Preretirement	L	L	L	L
Active oldsters	L	L	L	L
The frail	L	L	L	L

activity commitments limited the growth of racquetball and have caused at least a temporary loss of promoted opportunities.

JOGGING

Until 1982, jogging and running were combined in market surveys as a single activity. The National Recreation Surveys did not include either in 1965, and Nielsen added jogging/running in 1979. Trend analysis, then, faces two problems. The first is that "jogging" as a form of exercise was not distinguished from "running" as a speed-and-distance-measured sport until recently. The second is that neither was recognized as a significant activity until the mid or late 1970s.

Long-term trends

Jogging is defined as exercise running at some pace faster than a walk but excluding competitive running. Interest in this on-demand activity seems to have developed gradually in the 1960s and early 1970s. Jogging often begins at the residential doorstep, and some joggers are on the streets and sidewalks year-round regardless of climate. Others make it a seasonal activity or move to an indoor track where available in winter climates. Some jog in small groups that meet for the purpose, and others usually do it alone. Most, however, do it according to personal schedules with little or no travel to a special site.

Most literature suggests that a west coast movement began in the 1960s and spread across the country, promoting jogging/running as noncompetitive exercise. The public nature of the activity combined with increased media attention gave the impression of a widespread wave of participation. Without reliable and comparable data, we can only generally estimate the activity life cycle. Following decades of low rates of jogging/running, a growth period seems to have occurred from about 1965 through the 1970s. The peak may have been reached by 1980. More recent data document the plateau curve.

Short-term trends

The Nielsen survey reports a reduction of 4 percent between 1979 and 1982. This is consistent with the SMS data. Unfortunately, the 1979 survey combines jogging and running as a designated category of activity and then separates them. The reduction from 15.8 percent in 1979 to 12.0 percent in 1982 can be ascribed partly to this change in categories. However, adding the 1.6 percent of runners to the jogging rate for 1982 still amounts to only 13.6 percent, more than 15 percent lower than the 1979 rate.

The declining trend is about the same for males and females: combined jogging and running rates for men declined from 16.9 percent in 1979 to 14.3 percent in 1982 and for women about 14.8 percent to 12.1 percent. The 1984 rates are insignificantly lower than those for 1982. The rates for 1985 are 14.8 percent for males and 12.2 percent for females. The plateau level may increase slightly over time.

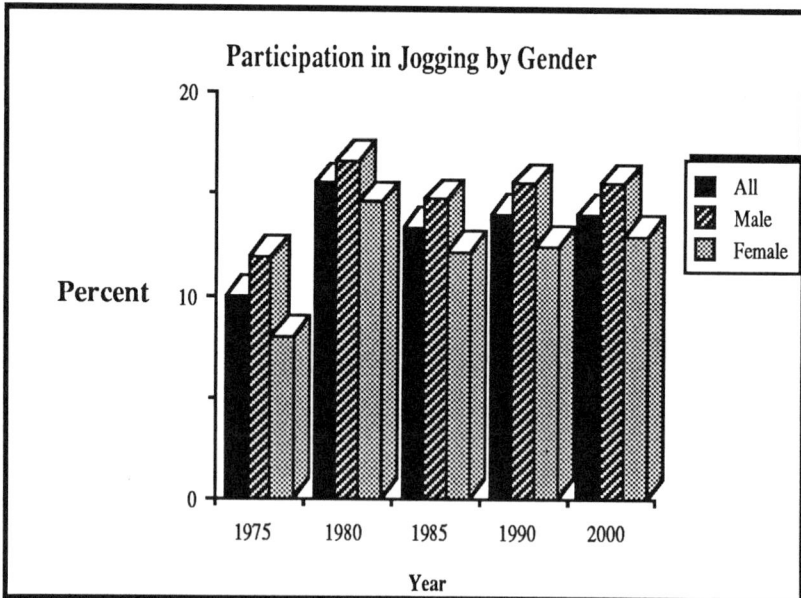

Participation in Jogging by Gender

This activity is low-cost, flexible in timetable, and self-paced. Frequency figures are especially interesting. Assuming that physical fitness and health are major motivating factors in this strenuous and sometimes painful activity, commitment measured by regularity is somewhat suspect. The MRI and SMS surveys for each year consistently show that about 30 percent of those who jogged did so at least once a week through the year. Conversely, 40 percent jogged 15 times or less. These figures are consistent with surveys of the readership of *Runners' World,* a group that would be presumed to be above average in commitment. Such frequency estimates suggest that some of the media figures about the number of joggers are suspect, especially when the number who jogged even once are translated into statements such as "X million Americans were out running this morning."

Some jogging is consistent and regular throughout the year, probably about 30 percent of the total. Some is sporadic and seasonal, perhaps related to preparation for a particular season or activity. Some is just occasional and intermittent

Cohort analysis

Jogging is strongly and inversely related to age. The percentage of joggers aged 18 to 24 is four times larger than that in the 55- to 64-year-old cohort.

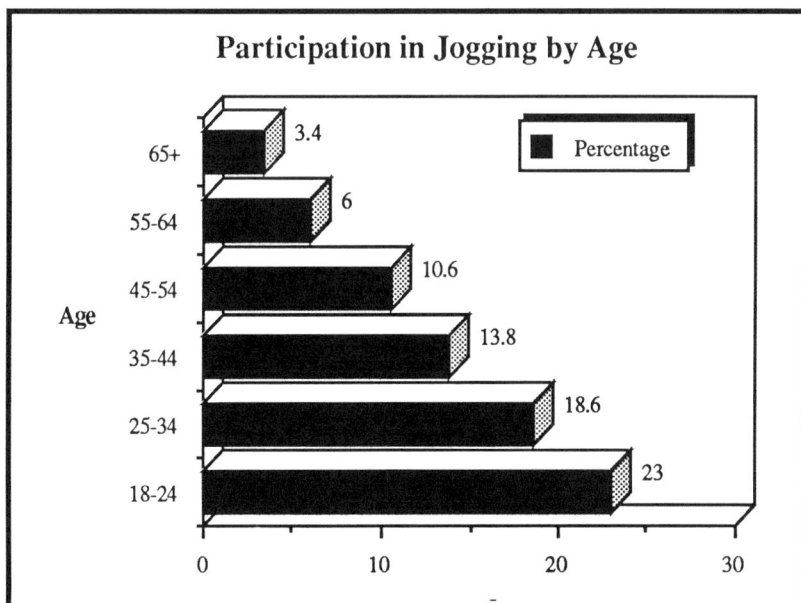

Participation in Jogging by Age

Cohort analysis, however, suggests that most of the reduced rates may have been among the youngest cohort. Participation rates for those aged 24 to 44 actually increased slightly but consistently from 1982 to 1985. For those younger and older, the rates decreased. This indicates that this age category, for whom time is a major constraint but physical fitness is still a concern, finds jogging a convenient way of achieving fitness goals. Since these categories include the "boomer" cohort, the decline from an earlier participation peak may be arrested. The plateau may even show a small but measurable increase if these younger Establishment period adults continue the activity.

Target markets

Age has already been identified as the key factor in participation rates, with a major drop-off in jogging after the age of 45. Since jogging is a low-cost activity, income would seem to have little impact. That may be the case, but the relationship of higher education to participation is strong. The correlation of education and income, however, yields a spurious relationship. Education indicates lifestyle that includes more readiness to engage in strenuous exercise to enhance health and appearance.

Participation in Jogging by Education and Income

Education	% Jogging
Less than HS grad	5.8
HS grad	9.4
Some college	16.7
College grad	18.6

Income	
-$10,000	6.5
$10-24,999	9.5
$25-34,999	15.3
$35-49,999	16.0
$50,000+	15.1

The percentages that jogged about once a week or more remained consistent at about 40 percent for all categories. When the student cohort — identified as having low incomes and "some college" — are excluded, then jogging emerges as an activity primarily for Discretionary men and women in their 20s, 30s, and early 40s for whom such exercise is part of an overall lifestyle.

Some combine jogging with other athletic participation, most often males who are conditioning themselves for another sport.

Future projections

Jogging participation has probably stabilized from the slight decline it experienced after peaking between 1976 and 1980. In fact, the slight increases for the important cohorts aged 25 to 44 suggest the possibility of a measured gain in participation. Recurrent injury from running regularly on hard surfaces has been a major concern, but improved equipment has reduced this constraint. Some jogger/runners may be switching to "low-impact" activities such as bicycling or at-home exercise equipment to avoid injury. For others, the commitment to this outdoor, on-demand, low-cost, and high-benefit activity remains strong.

RECREATION TARGET MARKETS: JOGGING

G = GROWTH MARKET P = POTENTIAL MARKET
E = ESTABLISHED MARKET L = LOW-PROBABILITY MARKET

Category	Low-end	Middle Mass	Discretionaries	High-end
Preparation	L	P	E	E
Free singles	L	P	G	G
Young parents	L	P	P	P
Established	L	L	P	P
Transitionals	L	L	P	P
Late singles	L	L	P	P
Preretirement	L	L	E	E
Active oldsters	L	L	P	L
The frail	L	L	L	L

DISTANCE RUNNING

Surveys have only distinguished distance running from jogging for a few years. Joggers usually measure time and distance in terms of quotas. They may take measures of aerobic indices of fitness. Runners combine time and distance measures such as "how far in a given time" or "how long for that distance."

Many enter competition and use the events as markers for performance. They are most likely to follow running as a sport, buy special equipment, and keep records.

There are no long-term trend data for distance running. As with jogging, the activity apparently began to "catch on" in the 1960s. It expanded through the 1970s and early 80s when various competitions and "fun runs" were promoted by both market-sector and public recreation providers. The 26+-mile Marathon is balanced somewhat by events of 5 or 10 kilometers that reflect international measurement systems and standards.

Short-term trends

The trend analysis is severely limited because data are available only since 1982. Furthermore, SMS gathered data somewhat differently in 1985. Distance running attracts considerably fewer participants than does noncompetitive jogging. Participation figures for organized events in many parts of the country have indicated that distance running may have peaked in the first half of the 1980s and then declined slightly. Such indirect measures are unreliable, although they are consistent with indications of slightly reduced participation for the youngest age cohort, those aged 18 to 24 from 1982 to 1984. When total participation is less than 2 percent or 3 percent of the adult population, a decline from 4 percent to 3.6 percent in the most active category would have noticeable impacts on special event participation.

The short-term trend is probably similar to that for jogging with a lag of about two years. The growth period was certainly the later 1960s and 1970s. A peak may have been reached by 1985. The plateau, however, is not expected to be much lower than the peak. Again, the SMS surveys report an increase in running participation for the key age groups between 25 and 44 years old. The relatively large "boomer" cohort seems most likely to continue running into their 40s or possibly even beyond, although at declining rates.

Frequency estimates for distance running, as expected, demonstrate a higher commitment level than for many less

Participation in Distance Running by Gender

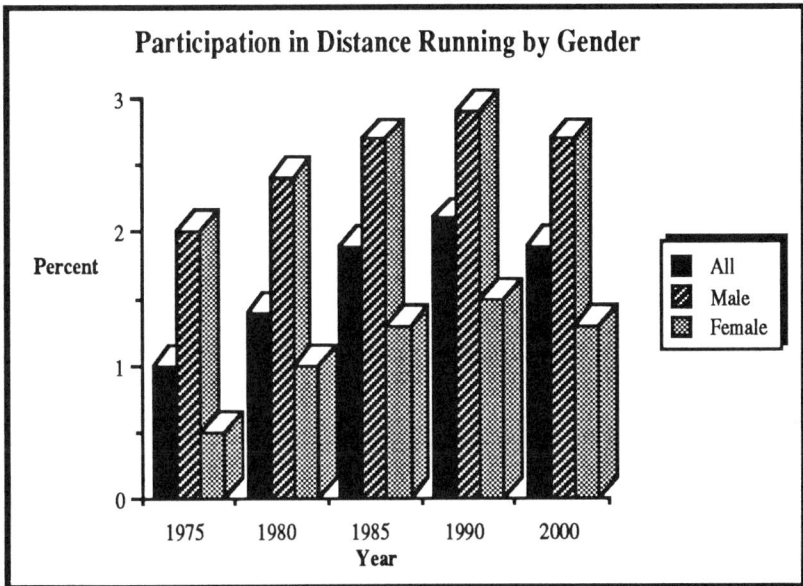

disciplined and demanding kinds of recreation activity. As many as 70 percent of those who run at all did so 15 times a year or more. At least 30 percent ran at least once a week. While it may be surprising to the devotees who run at least three to four times a week, these are high percentages in terms of recreational regularity for American adults. Although only 0.5 percent to 1 percent of American adults may run as often as once a week, that is a significant number for such a demanding activity. The meaning of "running" for those who do so only a few times a year, on the other hand, seems problematic.

Cohort analysis

Runners tend to be young. As they age, some runners might even slow down and become joggers. Therefore, the age of 40 seems to be the magic point at which running diminishes. There is, however, a persistent cadre of older runners.

Interestingly, the percentage of older participants who run once a week or more may be higher than for the younger cohorts. Running is a special kind of activity combining low cost with ease of access and scheduling and high demands in terms of regularity and effort. Runners may be divided between those who are committed to running itself as distinct from younger athletes who run to condition themselves for other sports and strenuous activities.

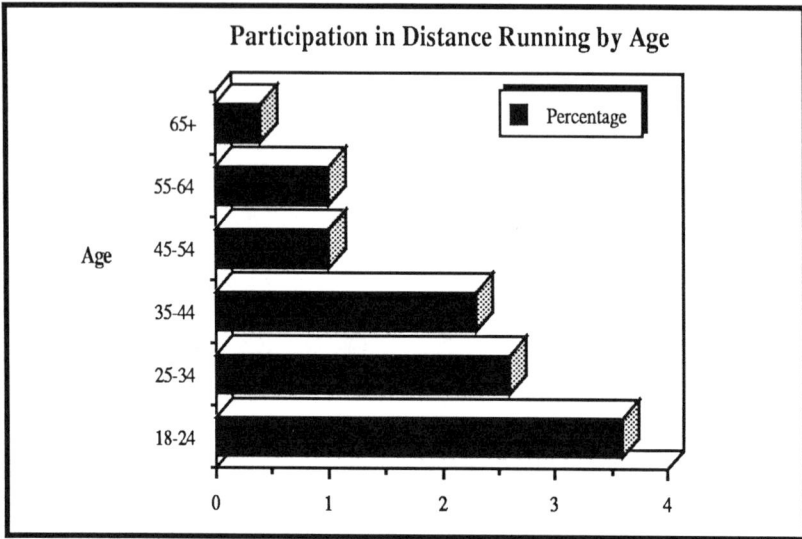

Participation in Distance Running by Age

Age	
65+	
55-64	
45-54	
35-44	
25-34	
18-24	

Target markets

Runners are most likely to be males, 2:1 over females, and under age 40. They also most often subscribe to a lifestyle with concern for long-term health, leisure and self-development, and that is indexed by higher levels of education.

As with jogging, income is most relevant in that it depends on education level. The cohort of students is significant: they are still in college, have low incomes, but run even though they tend to have many alternatives. Running comes into prominence more for those who have completed college and must develop a pattern of physical activity without access to school programs.

The costs of running are primarily those of time, effort, and discipline. Although shoes can be relatively expensive, the costs are nothing like those of downhill skiing, another relatively elite activity. Requirements for participation center around commitment, health, and vigor rather than on blocks of free time or high income. Such attributes tend to be associated with college-educated individuals under age 40 with values and interests that include physical achievement.

Participation in Distance Running by Education

Education	% Running
Less than HS grad	1.4
HS grad	1.4
Some college	2.4
College grad	3.7

Future projections

The peak for competitive running may be past, but distance-and-speed-measured running is not about to fade away. Although some participants fall away due to injuries, competing interests, or age-related changes, they are likely to be replaced by others who maintain such strenuous activity in their post-school years. If retention rates are strong among "boomers," the next decade may see a slight participation increase in running followed by another small decline. The plateau should be only a little below the peaks.

RECREATION TARGET MARKETS: RUNNING

G = GROWTH MARKET   P = POTENTIAL MARKET
E = ESTABLISHED MARKET   L = LOW-PROBABILITY MARKET

Category	Low-end	Middle Mass	Discretionaries	High-end
Preparation	L	E	E	E
Free singles	L	E	E	E
Young parents	L	L	P	P
Established	L	L	G	G
Transitionals	L	L	P	P
Late singles	L	L	P	P
Preretirement	L	L	E	E
Active oldsters	L	L	L	L
The frail	L	L	L	L

ICE-SKATING

The most significant factor in ice-skating has been its geographical location. It was strictly for northern climates with long periods of cold weather. Indoor rinks, especially for hockey and figure skating, have changed that somewhat. There are several kinds of skating: informal skating on ponds and in the free periods of rinks, competitive sports including racing and hockey, and figure skating. The styles are segregated by age as well as by household income and region.

Long-term trends

The Nielsen surveys report a 4 percent increase in skating participation from 1973 to 1976 followed by a 26 percent reduction from 1976 to 1979 and a 5 percent loss from 1979 to 1982. While the shift for the period from 1976 to 1979 seems exaggerated, declining rather then increasing participation is indicated in the 1970s.

Short-term trends

The SMS data do not indicate increases in participation.

Cohorts of ice-skating participants who are now in their 30s and 40s seem to be continuing with skating although at reducing rates. The cohort, on the other hand, shows the greatest rate of reduction in skating. The short-term trends and projections suggest slightly lower rates of skating participation. Skating participation is dispersed across all middle-income categories and is only weakly related to education level.

Frequency divides occasional "social" skaters from those committed to some type of ice-skating. Over 80 percent of those who skated did so ten times or less. Only about 3 percent of skaters were on the ice once a week or more often. In this case, the 20-80 rule is probably more like a 5-95 division in markets.

Participation in Ice Skating According to Age and Gender			
Age	1979	1982	1985
18 to 24	9.1	8.4	5.6
25 to 34	5.9	6.4	4.9
35 to 44	4.7	4.1	2.9
45 to 54	2.7	1.9	1.7
55 to 64	1.2	1.2	1.1
65+	.6	1.1	.8
Gender			
Male	4.6	4.6	3.4
Female	4.4	3.9	3.0

Target markets

Not included in these data are those under the age of 18 years who are engaged in youth hockey, figure skating classes, and other organized skating programs. They would seem to be the major market even though few will continue their participation into adult years. The high cost of indoor facilities and seasonal fluctuations in outdoor conditions are limiting factors for this activity. It is possible, however, that latent markets may rise among childrearing families who can share the activity. Because cost and climate factors limit this activity, no dramatic increase in adult participation is likely in this century. The downward trend might be halted as current youth skaters enter adult life course periods, but they are more likely to change to other kinds of recreation.

SWIMMING

The activity category of swimming includes a variety of environments: public pools, residential pools, lakes, ocean beaches, and rivers. It also encompasses a variety of styles from competition to play and from swimming laps for conditioning to card games on the poolside deck. Swimming participation declines with age, but there is no age group that does not swim. As a result of this variety, swimming is one of the most stable activities. Particular sites may lose markets as older pools become shabby, beaches are polluted, or more attractive sites are developed. Swimming, however, as an activity remains at the top in attracting interest and participation.

Long-term Trends

The National Recreation Surveys report relative stability from 1965 to 1983: 51 percent to 56 percent for males and 45 percent to 51 percent for females. The overall moderage growth in participation comes from those over age 25, and the greatest percentage of increase occurs among the categories aged 40 and over.

The Nielsen surveys indicate relative stability with a drop of 3 percent from 1973 to 1976, a gain of 2 percent from 1976 to 1979, and a loss of 3 percent from 1979 to 1982. All those differences are within sampling error margins and suggest that rates of swimming in the 1970s did not change.

Short-term trends

The same pattern is indicated by the SMS surveys. Total participation is stable at 31 percent with male participation declining slightly between 1979 and 1985 from 33.3 percent to 32.7 percent and female participation rising from 29.8 percent to 31.3 percent. All parallel data sources are consistent with both these percentages and the trends.

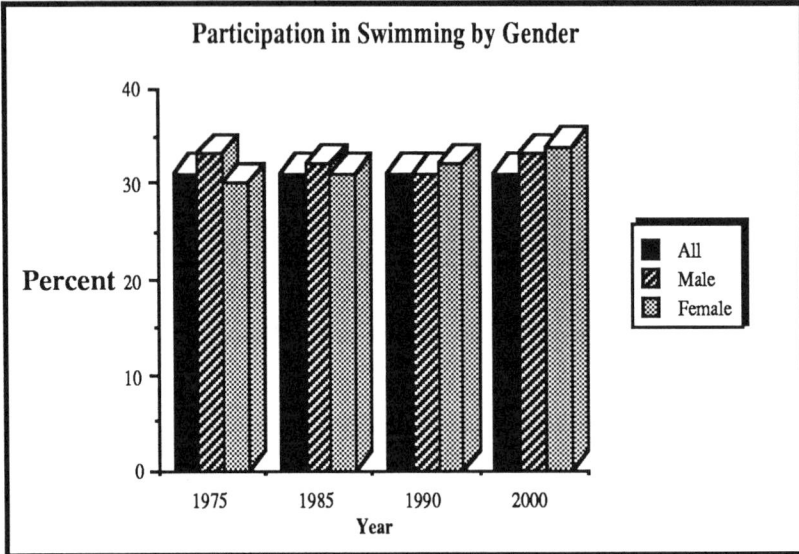

Participation in Swimming by Gender

Percent (y-axis: 0, 10, 20, 30, 40)

Years: 1975, 1985, 1990, 2000

Legend: All, Male, Female

Frequency for swimming is seasonal in some climates so that yearly frequencies vary. In general, about 40 percent of those who reported swimming at all did so fewer than ten times in a year, 35 percent swam 11 to 23 times, 15 percent swam 24 to 59 times, and 10 percent swam 60 or more times according to the SMS data. Swimming, then, is an occasional and seasonal activity for 60 to 80 percent of the third of the adult population that swim at all. Then there are those who may swim every day during a vacation and seldom, if ever, at any other time. No more than 20 percent of all adult swimmers, or 6 percent of the adult population, swim regularly all year.

Cohort analysis

While children and youth have the highest rates of swimming, there is no age group that does not swim at all. The reservation of many public and private pools for adult swimming in the early evening supports the extension of markets to all physically able age categories. Those aged 25 to 34 swim just as much as those aged 18 to 24. Rates remain substantial for those in their 40s, 50s, and 60s. In fact, the greatest percentage of increase from 1979 to 1985 was among the 55- to 64-year-old group, from 15.2 percent to 19.0 percent.

Participation in Swimming by Age

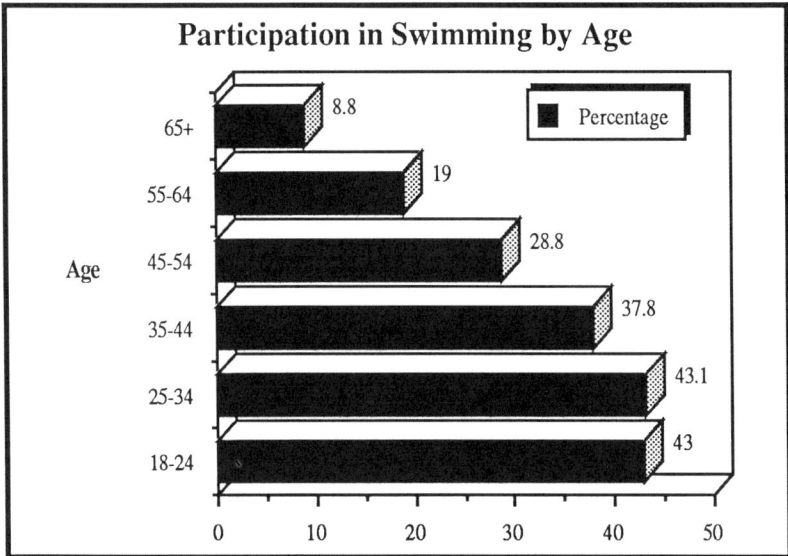

There is no indication of dramatic change among age cohorts. Both long- and short-term trends suggest slight but consistent increases in swimming among those in Establishment and Pre-retirement periods of the life course. This trend may be based on greater numbers of vacations taken near water resources as well as support for swimming as a desirable activity for those in middle years.

Target markets

Those in the lowest education and income categories are less than half as likely to swim as the rest of the population, showing a consistent correlation of education and income levels to swimming. Styles of swimming may vary more than general rates. Swimming in private residential pools and indoor pools as well as in exclusive vacation locales is more income-based than swimming in public pools and accessible urban beaches. There may also be a crossing pattern with age: education and income level are more predictive of swimming for those in the older age categories. Except for those from low-income households, children and youth may swim in less status-related patterns.

Only the poor are really excluded from swimming in a dramatic fashion. The other differences reflect access to opportunities through the life course: those most able to travel, purchase access to more attractive facilities, and have learning opportunities — that is, those of middle and higher incomes — are most likely to swim at any age.

Participation in Swimming by Education and Income

Education	% Swimming
Less than HS grad	15.0
HS grad	31.5
Some college	43.5
College grad	45.3

Income	
-$10,000	14.4
$10-24,999	32.7
$25-34,999	41.0
$35-49,999	41.6
$50,000+	43.2

Future projections

No dramatic changes are indicated away from this long-term stability in swimming participation. The gradual increase in rates

RECREATION TARGET MARKETS: SWIMMING

G = GROWTH MARKET   P = POTENTIAL MARKET
E = ESTABLISHED MARKET   L = LOW-PROBABILITY MARKET

Category	Low-end	Middle Mass	Discretionaries	High-end
Preparation	P	E	E	E
Free singles	P	E	E	E
Young parents	L	E	G	E
Established	L	P	G	E
Transitionals	L	P	G	E
Late singles	L	P	G	E
Preretirement	L	P	G	G
Active oldsters	L	L	G	G
The frail	L	L	L	L

among those in their 40s, 50s, and 60s suggests the possibility of more swimmers among the "boomer" cohort and somewhat greater demand for adult opportunities in the remainder of this century. In general, participants will be prepared to incur higher financial costs for superior access and quality. Water resources will remain a major component of vacation locale appeal.

TENNIS

Tennis is a relatively ancient activity that has experienced periods of boom, peak, and decline. It is now in a plateau of its activity life cycle. It can be played at a variety of levels in skill and competitive orientation. In its common form, however, it is a competitive racquet sport in which the acquisition and demonstration of skill is central to participants.

Long-term trends

Tennis increased dramatically in participation during the 1970s. The NRS show the participation growth from 7 percent to 18 percent for males and 6 percent to 31 percent for females from 1965 to 1983. The Nielsen surveys indicate an increase in numbers of tennis players of 45 percent from 1973 to 1976 and 10 percent from 1976 to 1979. The peak had been reached by 1980, however, and a 21 percent reduction ensued between 1979 and 1982. The "tennis boom" had come and gone. The question is the level of the post-peak plateau.

Short-term trends

The SMS surveys report a decline in tennis participation from 1976 through 1985. That decline, however, is slowing. In fact, it is likely that the plateau rates of participation have nearly been reached.

The Simmons surveys show a reduction for males of 6 percent from 1976 to 1979, 35 percent from 1979 to 1982, and 15 percent from 1982 to 1985. The same declining trend for females is 6 percent, 19 percent, and 30 percent for the respective years. The period 1980 to 1982 consistently shows marked reduction in tennis participation. Then in the mid-80s, the rate of decline levels

Participation in Tennis by Gender

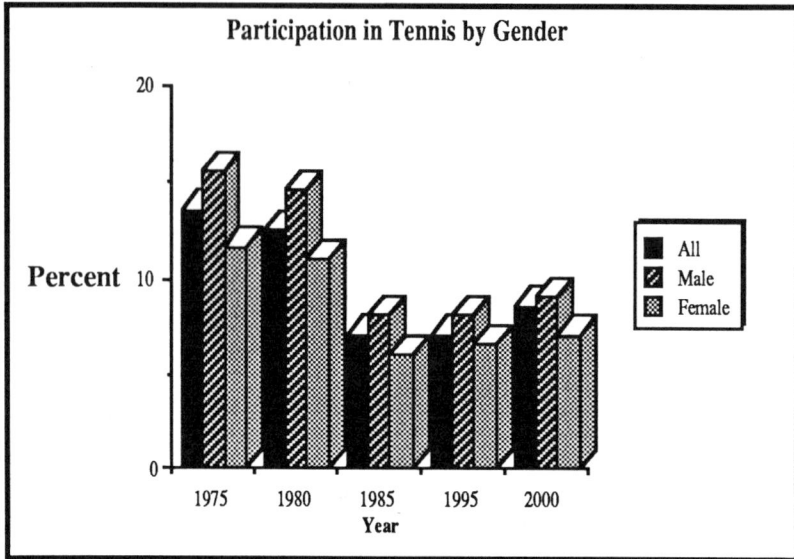

It is likely that the plateau rates of participation have nearly been reached.

The Simmons surveys show a reduction for males of 6 percent from 1976 to 1979, 35 percent from 1979 to 1982, and 15 percent from 1982 to 1985. The same declining trend for females is 6 percent, 19 percent, and 30 percent for the respective years. The period 1980 to 1982 consistently shows marked reduction in tennis participation. Then in the mid-80s, the rate of decline levels and may be moving toward relative stability, especially for males.

Frequency rates are similar to other physically strenuous recreation activities. Of those who played at all in 1985, 50 percent did so fewer than ten times. About 12 percent played once a week or oftener throughout the year. Again, a fair estimate taking account of seasonality would be that 20 to 30 percent of all players played as often as once a week in season. The SMS trend data indicate that as the overall number who play goes down, the percentage who play at least ten times a year increases. This indicates that the losses have occurred primarily among casual players and dabblers, while those who have invested in gaining reasonable skills may be participating at about the same rates.

Participation in Tennis by Age

Legend: ■ Percentage

Age categories (vertical axis): 65+, 55-64, 45-54, 35-44, 25-34, 18-24

Horizontal axis: 0, 2, 4, 6, 8, 10, 12

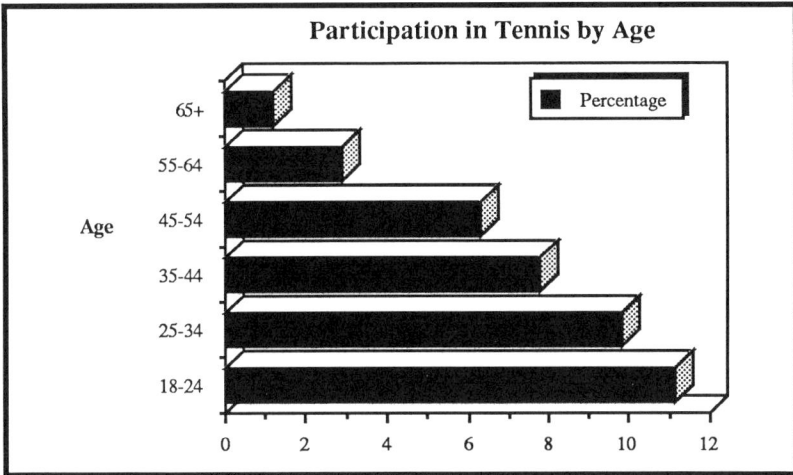

Cohort analysis

Tennis may be played at varying levels of ability and exertion. It is, however, a demanding competitive sport. As such, older cohorts are much less likely to play than younger.

The younger cohorts, however, are those among whom the post-peak decline is most marked. For tennis players over age 45, there is no significant reduction in the 1980s. Those who have committed themselves to some level of skill-acquisition in adult years seem most likely to go on playing.

Target markets

The cohort analysis suggests a target market among those in their middle and later adult years who play tennis at more than a beginning level. This implies that a threshold level of skill produces satisfaction. As with other long-handled racquet sports, that threshold may cause many beginners to drop out, but it enhances retention for those who reach an adequate skill level.

As with other activities that can be played at moderate cost on public sites and without highly expensive equipment, the markets are indexed more by education level than income.

The declines in participation seem to be most consistent for those in the middle ranges of both education and income, though without any clearcut shift in segmentation. The market segment of greatest retention would seem to be men and women in their 40s and 50s with college degrees who have invested in gaining a viable level of skill. The major questions are the rates at which those in their teens and 20s are taking up the activity and the persistence of the "boomer" cohort as they move into and through their middle years.

Future projections

The decline from the late 1970s peak in tennis participation seems to have ended. The major question is whether the plateau will be stable or if it will enter a period of gradual market growth. For long-term growth, at least 15 percent of those in their teens and 20s will have to stay with the sport long enough to gain a satisfying skill level. Shorter-term stability and

Participation in Tennis by Education and Income

Education	% Tennis
Less than HS grad	2.6
HS grad	4.8
Some college	10.8
College grad	15.8

Income	
-$10,000	3.5
$10-24,999	4.8
$25-34,999	10.2
$35-49,999	12.0
$50,000+	13.6

RECREATION TARGET MARKETS: TENNIS

G = GROWTH MARKET   P = POTENTIAL MARKET
E = ESTABLISHED MARKET   L = LOW-PROBABILITY MARKET

Category	Low-end	Middle Mass	Discretionaries	High-end
Preparation	P	P	E	E
Free singles	P	P	E	E
Young parents	L	L	G	E
Established	L	L	G	E
Transitionals	L	P	G	E
Late singles	L	L	P	E
Preretirement	L	L	P	E
Active oldsters	L	L	E	E
The frail	L	L	L	L

even slight growth depends on the "boomers" and the extent to which they go on playing tennis in their 30s, 40s, and even 50s. In general, a period of overall stability seems most likely.

PAINTING, DRAWING, AND SCULPTING

Producing works of graphic and plastic art is most often done at home. Classes for acquiring and improving skills as well as special facilities for ceramics and sculpting are generally offered by public, private, and market-sector providers in the community. Such art production, then, is both an at-home and a community activity.

Long-term trends

No long-term survey data exist. There is some basis for estimating that such activity increased during the 1960s and into the 1970s because it is related to higher education levels and is engaged in by both women and men. The 1960s and early 1970s was a time in which the increase of women in the work force, while consistent, was not as dramatic as in the later 1970s and early 1980s. Thus a substantial cohort of college-educated women in the post-war period were likely to have had both the time and interest to engage in artistic production.

Short-term trends

More recently, however, is a counter-trend of increasing percentages of women employed outside the home, especially those of traditional childrearing age. Even though education levels of each cohort are higher than the one before, this major market segment for artistic activity has known a sharp decrease in available time.

A second factor may be the increased participation in more physical activities by the same cohort of women. In any case, the short-term participation trends in painting, drawing, and sculpting are down. The increased interest and skill that might be derived from higher education levels has been countered by competition for time for work or other kinds of activity. One noteworthy trend is that the participation reductions have been less for men than women: 20 percent for men and 40 percent for women from 1979 to 1985. The gender difference, then, is decreasing. By 1985 it was only 5.2 percent for males versus 7.7 percent for females.

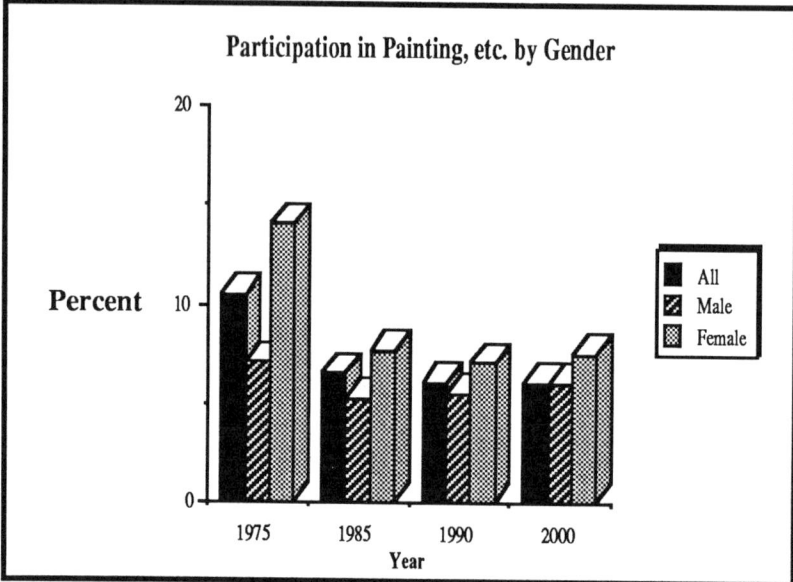

Participation in Painting, etc. by Gender

Percent (vertical axis, 0 to 20)

Legend:
- All
- Male
- Female

Year (horizontal axis): 1975, 1985, 1990, 2000

Frequency rates for such activity are consistent with the 20-80 rule. About 20 percent engage in such activity at least once a week and 60 percent paint or draw or sculpt fewer than ten times a year.

Cohort analysis

Age appears to be more a cohort factor than an index of ability. Those in school are most likely to engage in such activity. On the other hand, rates do not differ significantly for those aged 35 to 64. The cohort pattern seems to illustrate college-related introduction followed by a reduction in artistic engagement when programs and facilities are less convenient and competing role requirements emerge. Then, those whose commitment is high enough continue a pattern that persists through most of the active adult periods of the life course. More and more, employment requirements seem to conflict with artistic interests to reduce participation.

Target markets

Painting, drawing, and sculpting are associated with education more than income. On the other hand, artistic production is less gender-differentiated than it was even a decade ago. This may reflect changing gender role definitions as well as increased female employment.

The percentages in the categories for "some college" and the lower income groups reflect those in the category aged 18 to 24 who are still in school and involved in arts programs offered there. Removing students would probably produce a higher correlation between education level and arts participation. A central target market, then, is those who began such engagement in school and found it satisfying enough to continue. Arts engagement more than any other kind of leisure is usually begun in school. Further, interest and skill levels are related to the number of years in school.

Participation in Painting, etc. by Education and Income	
Education	% Painting,etc.
Less than HS grad	4.3
HS grad	6.8
Some college	8.2
College grad	7.7
Income	
-$10,000	4.8
$10-24,999	7.3
$25-34,999	6.7
$35-49,999	6.4
$50,000+	6.7

Future projections

Two factors are opposed in projecting trends. With a higher proportion of women in the labor force, time available for demanding arts disciplines is reduced. Such engagement at home, however, can be scheduled to fit other timetables. On the other hand, each cohort of both men and women is more likely to have attended and completed college. Current trends suggest that male participation will level off and female engagement will continue to decline, but at a lower rate. As with any activities that demand high levels of skill for maximum satisfaction, the key is the commitment level. Unless school programs intensify that commitment for those who attend college, increased artistic production for recreation in this century is unlikely. On the other hand, the dramatic drop in participation, especially by women, can be expected to diminish, especially for those entering their post-parental life course periods.

RECREATION TARGET MARKETS: PAINTING, ETC.			
G = GROWTH MARKET P = POTENTIAL MARKET E = ESTABLISHED MARKET L = LOW-PROBABILITY MARKET			
Category	Low-end	Middle Mass	Discretionaries	High-end
Preparation	L	P	E	E
Free singles	L	L	P	P
Young parents	L	L	P	G
Established	L	L	E	E
Transitionals	L	L	E	E
Late singles	L	L	G	P
Preretirement	L	L	G	P
Active oldsters	L	L	G	P
The frail	L	L	L	L

OTHER COMMUNITY-BASED ACTIVITIES

Few trend data are available for seven activities. Nevertheless, the market surveys provide valuable indications of the extent and composition of current markets.

Billiards and Pool

These two table games have been traditionally male activities. They differ, however, in their most common locales. Billiards tends to be played in upper-class private homes and clubs. Pool, on the other hand, is associated with urban working class parlors. "Snooker," a British version of pool, has attracted a television audience that seems to have expanded interest. Combining the two types of games makes the market segmentation rather uncertain. It is similar to calling show jumping and quarterhorse racing both "horseback riding."

Participation in billiards and pool is still predominately male: 17.3 percent to 7.0 percent of adult females. Although lacking any strenuous physical requirements, both games also tend to be played by the young. This is especially the case for pool in urban halls.

Percentages by Age in Pool/Billiards	
Age	Rate
18 to 24	24.1
25 to 34	16.8
35 to 44	11.4
45 to 54	7.5
55 to 64	4.4
65+	1.6

Since any such steep age-related decline is unlikely in billiards playing by high-income males, the inverse age correlation may reflect the pool hall segment of participation. Frequency follows the usual patterns. Of the 11.5 percent of the population aged 18 and over who engage in the activity, 67 percent do so less than ten times a year. About 15 percent play billiards or pool once a week or more.

The education and income breakdowns are of little use because of combined data, and there is no pattern of correlation by income levels. Somewhat surprisingly, those who have attended college are more likely to play than those who have not. This suggests that billiards and pool are played in quite different venues by different market segments. The present and future markets for this activity are varied and segmented. The activities have a long history, well-established demand, and the likelihood of continuation at some viable levels. On the other hand, their central market segments — working class urban youth for pool and elite urban males for billiards — are not growing segments of the population.

Dancing at Nighclubs and Discos

As with some other generic categories, combining a variety of styles and venues for the category obscures segmentation of the markets. Night clubs can be quite costly and limited to upper-income individuals. Discos and other dance facilities may vary widely in cost and ambience. Clearly, though, when all the forms of dancing outside the home are lumped together, the "activity" has substantial participation.

In 1984, 21.6 percent of the population 18 and over engaged in some kind of dancing at special locales (MRI). Females were slightly more likely to do so: 22.4 percent versus 20.6 percent for males. Frequency is varied: 65 percent danced ten times or less in a year, 24 percent danced between 11 and 41 times, and 11 percent danced 42 times or more.

Income is not a good predictor for dancing at clubs because of the number of younger people also included in the activity. Age and education, however, are significant.

Participation in Dancing by Education and Age

Education	% Dancing
Less than HS grad	12.4
HS grad	22.2
Some college	30.1
College grad	27.3
Age	
18 to 24	37.2
25 to 34	31.6
35 to 44	21.5
45 to 54	15.7
55 to 64	9.6
65+	4.3

The major markets for such dancing opportunities are young, often the singles who use the activity for dating, meeting, and entertaining others. They tend to have completed high school, and, in fact, the single largest market segment is students. But persistent markets of older adults also maintain interest in some form of dance or night club locales for being with peers.

Dancing is thoroughly established as a major weekend evening activity for teens and young adults. The current forms and patterns of dance are significant symbols of peer-group identification and participation. These markets will continue to be strong even when the particular styles of dance and clubs change. The demand from adults further along in the life course diminishes: it tends to be low to occasional for most parental and establishment adults. Such locales may, however, attract increased participation from the transitional adults without stable marriages and who are re-entering the noncouple and extra-residential social scene.

Outdoor Concerts and Plays

Attending outdoor concerts and plays is an NRS activity category because of the "outdoor" aspect. The data, however, are not detailed enough to assess trends.

The long-term trend from 1965 to 1983 is one of increase: from 11 percent to 25 percent for males and from 12 percent to 26 percent for females. The gain was spread almost evenly across age categories: from 21 percent to 34 percent for ages 12 to 24, from 17 percent to 29 percent for ages 25 to 39, from 13 percent to 22 percent for ages 40 to 59, and from 9 percent to 12 percent for age 60+. Only those near or at retirement age increased their demand less than the standard of about 40 percent during the 18-year period.

Growth in participation in outdoor concerts depends largely on opportunities. There are, of course, a variety of styles. Youth and young adults are the market for rock concerts, and adolescents and younger couples for pop. Adults with some higher education are the major market for drama and classical music concerts, although classical music markets are not as age-differentiated as the pop-rock varieties. The education levels of the "boomer" cohort promises some growth in markets for attractive outdoor theatre and classical music for the remainder of this century. As the "GI Bill" cohorts increased markets in the 1960s and 70s, so their "baby boom" will add further to the demand in the 1990s.

Picnics

What could be more classical family recreation than the picnic? Picnics, backyard barbeques, and other such events are the staple for family and friends on summer weekends. It is somewhat surprising, then, to find that picnics are one of the very few kinds of recreation activity with a long-term trend of reduced participation.

NRS data indicate a reduction from 55 percent to 45 percent for males and from 59 percent to 51 percent for females. The decline may reflect the reduction in the proportion of the population with young children, and this is supported by the trend data by age group.

132

Picnicking is only slightly related to income or education level for those with high school education or more. Despite the reduction, picnics rank with swimming, walking, and reading in the near-universality of their participation. The market, however, is concentrated among family groups, especially those with children. Alternative picnics are those scheduled by a community or work-related organization. These picnics are social events in which the

Participation in Picnickingby Age		
Age	1965	1984
12 to 24	72	52
25 to 39	71	59
40 to 59	58	46
60+	36	29

outdoor locale and even the food and drink are stages for interaction.

Future projections depend largely on fertility and the extent of the childrearing period of the life course. The reduction in both suggests that picnic participation will continue to decline gradually. It remains, however, a broad-based activity that offers satisfactions central to the lifestyle of many households and families. Further, the larger proportion of single-parent families offers a growing market for this low-cost opportunity for interaction outside the home.

"Barbeques" might be classified as backyard picnics with a grill. Some of the old "picnic in the park" may have been transferred to the at-home setting. The Mediamark data report that men and women participated in barbeques more or less equally in 1984: 32.1 percent of males and 30.7 percent of females. About 55 percent did so ten times or less. Attending and having barbeques is a part of home-centered leisure styles for many adults. Those who have graduated from college participate at the rate of 41.7 percent. Along with those with incomes over $30,000, they are the most active market segments. They are, of course, most likely to have detached homes or other housing with space and facilities for a barbeque. Nor are barbeques limited to a single age category.

This age analysis indicates clearly that parental and other Establishment period adults provide the greatest demand for barbeque events and equipment. Middle mass and Discretionary

Participation in Barbequing by Age	
Age	% Barbequing
18 to 24	34.2
25 to 34	40.5
35 to 44	39.9
45 to 54	31.5
55 to 64	25.0
65+	10.4

families are the core of participation. Trends that suggest a possible stabilization or even a reduction in participation are shorter childrearing life course periods, an increase in families residing in multiple-unit housing, and more childless adults.

Roller skating

Roller skating includes both indoor and outdoor participation. No long-term trend data are available, but the SMS and MRI data are consistent for the period since 1979.

The early 1980s witnessed a technological advance in roller skates. The old metal wheels for outdoor skating were replaced with new composition wheels that permitted safer and quieter skating and more control. This caused a modest upsurge in participation betweeen 1979 and 1982, from 6.4 percent to 8.2 percent of the population aged 18 and over. By 1985, however, this rate had dropped back to 6.0 percent. Frequency is spread from the 3 percent who skated over 50 times to over 80 percent who skated ten times or less in a year.

Roller skating participants can be segmented by gender, age, and education level rather than by income level.

The demonstrated market segments for roller skating are pre-teens; teens, especially females; and students. About 60 percent of the market has consistently been female. College students and others just out of their teens are the major post-high school market. The market for adults is gradually declining through all the age categories, though. Any major market growth in the future seems unlikely if the improved wheel technology has already exhausted its impact. But warm-weather outdoor skating could attract some lower-income participants as new equipment costs come down. Areas with long warm seasons are critical opportunities as well as

Participation in Roller Skating by Education, Gender, and Age	
Education	% Roller Skating
Less than HS grad	5.1
HS grad	7.9
Some college	9.0
College grad	6.8
Gender	
Male	5.6
Female	8.5
Age	
18 to 24	14.6
25 to 34	10.7
35 to 44	7.2
45 to 54	3.2
55 to 64	2.1
65+	1.3

trend setters for this activity. In southern California, outdoor roller skating has attracted considerable participation in lower-income and ethnic neighborhoods. But most likely, the surge spurred by the improved equipment has peaked. Data for 1985 indicate decreased skating in the 18- to 24-year-old category, suggesting the possibility of further decline.

Outdoor Team Sports

Outdoor team sports such as softball are a staple in most public recreation programs. In more recent years, the traditional sports have been augmented by soccer and other imports, especially in the Northeast and on the West Coast.

Data are difficult to interpret because of inconsistency. The National Recreation Surveys lumped the sports together in some years and included a group aged 12 and above. The market surveys have been slow to add sports with growing participation and do not include participants under age 18. Amid such inconsistency, however, a general picture of stability seems to emerge, although it varies from one community to another depending on the resources and promotion of the local programs.

The Nielsen surveys separate baseball and softball. Baseball shows an increase of 3 percent from 1973 to 1976, a decrease of 4 percent from 1976 to 1979, and a larger loss of 10 percent from 1979 to 1982. These figures consistently demonstrate a steady trend of reduced adult participation in baseball beginning in the mid-1970s.

Softball trends are stable following steady increases during the 1970s: a 3 percent increase from 1973 to 1976, a 4 percent gain from 1976 to 1979, and a 1 percent loss from 1979 to 1982.

Participation in seasonal outdoor team sports has been concentrated primarily among males, although gender ratios differ by sport. For youth soccer and softball, for instance, the female participation rates have increased as opportunities were extended. This trend is expected to continue into post-school years as more female students engage in team sports.

The age-related declines in team sport participation come at two periods. The first occurs on leaving school when the times and places for competition that were facilitated are no longer available. The second, for those who have retained regular participation, seems to occur between age 35 and 45, as injuries and other physical limitations become a problem.

The SMS data cover four of the most common team sports and point to the same market segments identified in the more general surveys.

Of the total 10.5 percent who said they participated in some sport other than those specifically included in the survey, about 27 percent did so 50 times or more during the year. About 20 percent of the 10.5 percent played one to four times, 20 percent played five to nine times, and the remaining 40 percent played from 10 to 49 times a year.

The following trends and projections seem to characterize adult

Participation in Various Outdoor Team Sports in 1985

Sport	Participation rate
Basketball	5.5
Football	3.2
Soccer	1.5
Softball/baseball	8.1
Volleyball	6.2
None of these	33.7
Do not know	51.8

136

participation in team sports:

1. Participation in team sports on a regular basis is highly age-related. For those no longer in school, participation drops off year by year, with a major decline coming for those aged 35 to 45.

2. Female participation in team sports in school has increased dramatically. Sports such as softball and volleyball can be expected to attract more post-school age female participation as opportunities are offered.

3. The introduction of imported sports such as soccer should bring about measured increases in participation by young adults as those who have invested in skill acquisition want to continue participation.

Some variations are evident when the sports are taken one by one. Softball has the largest following with little market

Percentages of the Market for Four Team Sports (SMS)			Softball/	
Category	Basketball	Football	Baseball	Volleyball
Gender				
Male	8.8	5.5	11.2	6.7
Female	2.7	1.2	5.3	5.7
Age				
18 to 24	12.3	11.0	14.9	12.8
25 to 34	8.0	3.0	12.8	8.8
35 to 44	4.8	1.8	8.6	6.3
45 to 54	2.5	1.4	4.5	3.3
55 to 64	2.0	1.2	2.4	1.3
65+	1.0	.9	.8	.9
Income				
-$10,000	5.0	2.8	5.7	4.2
$10-24,999	6.5	4.8	8.5	5.5
$25-34,999	5.7	4.3	9.3	7.3
$35-49,999	5.7	4.1	9.6	7.4
$50,000+	4.9	3.5	9.5	7.1

differentiation by education or income. Basketball, on the other hand, attracts the largest percentage of players with low incomes and without high school diplomas. This obviously reflects the status of the game in inner-city ethnic areas. Volleyball is most likely to have the most female participants, and football and basketball the least.

One slightly confounding element may be that some of those claiming to be active in these sports in their 30s, 40s, and 50s may be doing so with their children. They may be referring to backyard, neighborhood, and even vacation participation or to their roles as coaches.

Future projections must incorporate some conflicting elements:

1. Lower overall projections as the cohorts entering their 20s become smaller.

2. More women who gained team sports skills in school in the last decade.

3. The likelihood that more Discretionaries will engage in active sports that do not require 10 to 20 players at a time.

4. The impact of less traditional sports.

5. Smaller families and consequent fewer "parental" engagements as backyard players and coaches.

On the other hand, such sports as softball seem to have gained a considerable and stable following. Both softball and volleyball may gain more in female players than they lose in the smaller cohorts of males in their 20s. Team sports are not experiencing rapid growth, but neither are they dying away. Some market shifts toward women and perhaps slightly upward in age can be expected. The long-term impact of youth programs for team sports should not be over-estimated as post-school-age participants continue to drop out of team sports at a regular rate.

SUMMARY: COMMUNITY-BASED RECREATION ACTIVITIES

Community-based recreation is so varied that generalizations are difficult. They range from the traditional team sports such as softball to children's transportation such as bicycling to a fitness-related adult lifestyle and all the on-demand activities such as jogging. There are public programs and facilities as well as those provided by the market sector. Sometimes they are in competition and sometimes one feeds participants to the other. They are the traditional family picnics and the newly-promoted upscale fitness centers.

Activities differ in their histories, current trends, composition of participants, and projections, and generalizations about "recreation" or "sports" simply cannot apply to each particular activity. Further, the history and opportunities in a specific community may run counter to national trends. Thus, generalizations are dangerous. Even so, a few that are based on demographic shifts may apply to several kinds of activity:

1. Females are more significant markets for active recreation.

2. Family activity remains important, but for shorter periods of the life course.

3. Concerns for health and fitness as well as for appearance are now established enough that adults in their 40s, 50s, and 60s are increasingly important markets for many kinds of relatively strenuous activity.

4. Climate is very important for many activities. In some cases, off-season alternatives are being sought as new markets for those who wish to maintain active recreation engagements all year.

5. Public recreation programs will be increasingly articulated with market-sector offerings to complement each other, rather than compete. Such complementarity involves resources such as ball diamonds as well as provisions for those who cannot afford up-market prices.

6. Community recreation providers will have to adjust to such economic shifts as 24-hour and 7-day work timetables and increased female participation in the labor force.

7. Cohort analysis is especially significant in looking ahead. Remember that every oncoming cohort has a higher percentage of college-educated members with somewhat different sets of expectations and recreation interests. Remember also that cohorts following the baby boom will be smaller.

8. Consider some conflicting factors: increased female employment versus higher education levels that produce interests in the arts, physical activity, and travel. Increasingly, the Discretionaries are limited by time rather than income. Both public and market providers will have to adust to time constraints.

9. Because of time pressures, activities that can be accomplished on one's own schedule rather than on some external timetable may win the most increased participation. Community recreation agencies may be called upon more and more to provide venues for activity rather than to provide organized programs.

AT-HOME
RECREATION

CHAPTER 5

This chapter will be limited to organized activity and will not include the most common at-home activities: watching television and videos, reading, talking with others in the household, informal play with children, walking, and activity around the yard. Some at-home activities, such as exercise for fitness, barbeques, and some painting and drawing, have already been analyzed in Chapter 4. And some other activities, such as jogging and running, are only home-based in that they begin and end at home.

The residence is the most common locale for leisure. The informal and accessible activities that predominate around the home are the "core" around which more extended activities are built. That core is daily, not occasional, and involves the companions who tend to be most central to our lives. Omitting such activity here is a matter of focus on those recreation activities that require provisions by the public and market sectors of the society, on "markets" and demand. And the core of regular leisure, so much of which is at home, occupies far and away the most time. According to one national study in the United States, 81 percent read for pleasure, 58 percent walked for pleasure, 88 percent watched television, 48 percent swam, 62 percent listened to the radio, 83 percent spent evenings with relatives regularly, and 65 to 75 percent engaged in sexual interaction. These are the regular contexts of leisure activity. Most of the organized activities discussed in this book are "special" rather than ordinary, highlights and punctuations rather than the common round of action and interaction.

There is also the problem of data. The federal government has concentrated on outdoor recreation resources. Marketing studies have included activities that require some provision of site or equipment by the market sector of the economy. Considerable at-home leisure falls between the cracks, neglected just because it is ordinary, low-cost, and requires no special purchases or travel. The point is that this book is about the kinds of recreation that call for provisions and providers, not the commonplace leisure that is a regular dimension of home life or even work life.

Cooking and Baking for Fun

We might not think of food preparation as recreation, but there is increasing interest in the preparation and serving of particular kinds of food and meals as leisure activity. More than just getting nourishment on the table, such cooking and baking is a special event, usually celebrated with and for others in and outside the household.

In the SMS surveys, 22.5 percent identified baking as a recreational activity and 15.9 percent said they had done some cooking for fun. The gender difference was not surprising: 9.8 percent of males and 34.0 percent of females for baking and 11.3 percent for males and 20.2 percent for females for fun cooking. Age is not a major factor, but those with college educations are about twice as likely to cook and bake as a leisure activity than those who have not graduated from high school.

Frequency figures suggest that such leisure-time kitchen activity is reserved for special occasions: about half of those reporting such activity engaged in it ten times or less in a year. About 20 to 25 percent engaged in cooking or baking for fun as often as once a week. This implies that such activity is often reserved for entertaining or for a special household meal.

Significant markets have been identified for equipment, ingredients, and literature that support leisure cooking and baking. They are usually labelled as "gourmet" or in some other way different from the daily kitchen tasks. This activity, then, differs in scheduling and motivation from the routines and satisfactions of the daily round. It yields the enjoyment of creating something special to be appreciated by significant other persons. And, it is quite consistent with the lifestyles of Discretionaries in the Establishment, Pre-retirement, and Active oldster phases of the life course. Projections of growth are positive.

Indoor Gardening and Raising Plants

Another growth activity at home has been the raising of small gardens and plants indoors. Partly a response to the increasing number of adults living in multiple-unit housing, 25.2 percent of the adult population participated in 1985. It is predominately a female activity: 35.0 percent versus 14.3 percent for males.

For some, indoor gardening is seasonal and may be related to preparation for outdoor planting. For most, however, it is a year-round activity that includes both caring for things that live and grow and enhancing the residential environment.

Indoor gardening and plant care is not differentiated by either income or education level, and there is also no age decline up to age 65. From age 25 through 64, about 28 percent of the adult population engages in such activity. Again, due to the increasing proportion of households expected to reside in apartments without access to private yards, such activity is likely to increase in the future.

Outdoor Gardening

Outdoor gardening is not a growth activity due to the smaller proportion of the adult population with easy access to suitable space. Gardening, however, continues to be an important at-home activity. In 1985, about 35 percent of the adult population did some outdoor gardening. For most, it was a regular engagement in season: only 36 percent of the 35 percent gardened ten days or less in the year, 30 percent gardened 42 days or more, and the remainder gardened between 11 and 41 days.

As with so many at-home activities, the participants are with few exceptions not significantly differentiated. The very poor and the very old and those under age 25 are less likely to garden. The peak ages are 35 to 64 with females only a little more likely to garden than men: 36.0 percent versus 33.8 percent.

Gardening can be quite simple and relatively low in cost if outdoor ground is available. It can also be quite expensive and elaborate. It may combine obligation and satisfaction for those who want to enhance their homes, outdoor surroundings, or provide some food. The future of gardening as a recreation activity depends primarily on one factor: access to suitable space. If multi-unit housing developments assign some private ground to occupants, then the reduction in detached homes with yards may not have as great an impact as might be expected. It is also possible that adult singles, single parents, and those in some time of transition will be less likely to invest their time and energy in a relatively isolated activity. Gardening will continue to attract those with the opportunity, especially in the Establishment and active later-life periods of the life course.

Playing Cards

Card playing has traditionally been a common social activity for adults. It is pursued about equally by men and women: 27.6 percent of males and 29.0 percent of females. Varieties of games and settings range from poker parlors to duplicate bridge tournaments and from commuter trains to campsites. Most card playing, however, is done at home and involves some entertaining.

Card playing is not consistently related to income or education level. Styles may differ, but the generic activity crosses most demographic lines. A gradual but consistent decline in card playing occurs with age, but adults of all ages play cards in significant numbers.

Frequency data indicate that card playing is an occasional activity for most. Of the 33.5 percent of adults who played during the year, over half played ten times or less. Under 20 percent played more than 42 times or about once a week.

Although card playing can be quite expensive, most studies suggest that the costs are adjusted to what players can afford. Poker limits or other stakes are designed to be noticeable, but not highly costly for groups that play together regularly. Often the financial stakes are primarily symbolic: penny-ante or 25 cents a round.

The future of such activity is less sure than some other at-home activity. The possibility of electronic entertainment taking up more time and reducing commitment to regular card playing is quite real. At-home entertainment, primarily on the TV screen and including cable and video is so accessible and relatively inexpensive that the social costs of organizing card games may be paid only by those really devoted to the activity. It is certainly not a form of at-home recreation that is likely to increase in participation.

Reading Books and Magazines

Reading remains a significant at-home activity. All the fears that television would produce a culture that did not read have proved unfounded. Reading for pleasure, however, does not usually involve great literature or difficult material. People read magazines, partly for entertainment and partly for useful information. They read newspapers, often skimming "hard news" and concentrating on features, human interest, and sports. They read mysteries and romance novels, "how-to" and self-help books. Most reading at home is recreational more than educational.

Nevertheless, 47 percent of the adult population did some reading of books and magazines for pleasure. Of that total, over half read at least once a week. Women are more likely to read than men: 53.9 percent versus 39.6 percent. Education level is one factor: 61.2 percent for college graduates, 53.9 percent for those with some college, 48.4 percent for high school graduates, and 33.6 percent for those without high school diplomas. Income does not differentiate readers significantly except at very low income levels. Within the 25- to 64-year-old age range, rates of reading are approximately equal.

Providing reading material is a major industry. Reading has provided choices somewhat lacking in regular television. Cable and video formats, however, do provide choices that could cut into some reading time. Most indications, however, are that reading is a thoroughly stable activity that is not likely to disappear. The major trend for the publishing industry is toward more market segmentation with types of material more directed toward particular population segments. The past two decades have also witnessed reading material becoming available for sale in all kinds of retail outlets from grocery stores to filling stations.

During the same period, public libraries have become "information centers" with a wide variety of new materials available for in-house use, for loan, and for rent.

Walking for Pleasure

Strictly speaking, walking may not be an at-home activity. It does, however, begin and end at the residence for most walkers most of the time. Walking is an activity with a variety of styles and purposes. People walk to get somewhere as well as simply to get out and about. They walk in couples and in groups, alone, and with animals. They walk around the neighborhood and on vacations, at a leisurely strolling pace and at a brisk conditioning clip. Children may walk because they have no choice. Adults usually walk because they do have a choice.

The long-term trend appears to be one of relative stability. The NRS shows slight increases from 1963 to 1983: from 43 percent to 45 percent for men and from 53 percent to 61 percent for women. Those aged 12 to 24 were found to walk considerably less, down from 67 percent to 57 percent. All other age categories increased, with the largest percentage being 36 percent to 42 percent for those aged 60 and over.

The college-educated walk almost twice as much as those who did not finish high school, 67 percent versus 35 percent. Income, probably as an indicator of lifestyle, is correlated with walking. Walking for most adults is a matter of choice rather than necessity.

Walking, then, is a recreational activity. Although there are no accurate short-term trend data, indications suggest that walking is on the increase for adults concerned about their health. Aerobic walking, regular and relatively brisk, is being promoted as an activity with many of the benefits of jogging, but without the impact injuries. Thus, walking as a regular activity will likely increase as the current cohorts in their 30s and 40s enter their 50s and 60s. They may seek special venues for walking in some locales, although the on-demand advantage of walking suggests that most will be from and back to the residence.

Summary: At-home activity

Recreation in and around the home is the core of adult leisure. It occupies far and away the most time. It is daily rather than occasional, common rather than special, and includes other persons central to our lives. It is out of this context that the special recreational engagements are chosen and developed. Even for the less common kinds of activity just introduced, age and socio-economic variations are relatively slight. At-home recreation continues throughout the life course for most adults, along with changes in activity and meaning related to marital status, the presence or absence of children, and ties to other social institutions. From the almost universal activity of watching television to more select activities such as disciplined exercise, access is easy. The opportunities do not require travel or meeting someone else's schedule. Further, most at-home activities are either cost-free or inexpensive.

This is not to say that there are no important markets created by at-home activity. Entertainment, equipment, apparel, learning opportunities including published material and video formats, and special facilities may be provided by market-sector providers. In fact, such at-home activity may offer more reliable markets than goods and service provision that require leaving home for special venues and programs.

The future projections for at-home leisure must take into account two significant impediments to growth. The first is space: more residences are being constructed to be space-efficient. If construction costs continue to rise, this trend may make dedicated space for at-home recreation increasingly rare. Designs allowing for multiple use will be necessary. The second counter-trend is familiar. Increased marital instability along with smaller family size suggest that fewer adults will have the social basis for interactive at-home leisure. Some traditional forms of leisure that require both space and family, the backyard picnic for example, may become less common.

On the other hand, the time and stress costs of metropolitan sprawl along with the difficulties of arranging recreation with others outside the household may place a premium on recreation in and around the home. Thus, more apartment complexes are being designed with recreation space included. There may be fewer backyards, but there may be more common pools, exercise rooms, and other facilities where residents can meet and engage in recreation on-site. Residential common space may replace the private space of the detached home for some kinds of leisure. Such provisions would respond to the greater numbers of adults who are in a marital transition or who will have long periods of singleness.

Residential leisure with some possible changing forms, then, is likely to remain significant for adults in the future. Important markets can be developed to widen the possibilities of recreation participation in and around the residence.

It's easy to get lost in the detail when we examine, even in summary form, the trends and projections for so many resource-based, community, and at-home recreation activities. The varied data sources, irregular trends, diversified target markets, and multi-factored futures are too much to remember. Chapters 3, 4, and 5 should be considered as reference sources rather than overall analyses. Even the summaries at the end of each chapter contain dimensions that are inconsistent with each other. Very seldom can projections for the year 2000 be made without a few "if" statements.

From this much data analysis, is there any overall picture? Can any generalizations be extracted from the foregoing activity-by-activity detail?

First, there are some general trends, although they may not be applicable to any particular community or even region without qualification. They are, however, worth noting.

Second, there are also some general warnings or limitations. Projections are not all on the same level of certainty. It is important to point out some of the limiting factors.

GENERAL TRENDS: CONTINUITIES AND CHANGES

More detailed continuities and changes were outlined in Chapter 2, and trends were summarized for each of the three kinds of activities at the end of each activity analysis chapter. Here we will move to a higher level of generalization.

Projections for Types of Activities

Resource-based outdoor recreation

The long-term trend toward increased participation in outdoor recreation that followed World War II has leveled. Overall, any continuing increases are occurring at declining rates. The economic impact of rising incomes along with improved and more widely available transportation has waned. Attention to natural environments has drawn some to resource-based recreation. And some recreation sites have become crowded.

Projections for the future focus on particular market segments that may increase participation. The large boomer cohort may be transferring from physically demanding activities to other styles of engagement with natural environments. Several factors indicate that future cohorts will travel more and remain more active in their 50s and 60s than those preceding. Adjustments to energy costs have been largely completed. The oncoming adult cohorts with their higher levels of education will likely travel and retain interests in resource-based recreation. Styles of participation may be more varied, especially since traditional family camping will be less common. Market-sector provisions will proliferate around recreation environments. Overall, demand for most kinds of outdoor recreation opportunities can be expected to grow slightly unless the economy fails to provide discretionary incomes for those entering their work career trajectories.

Community-based recreation

Some traditional community sports are not increasing in popularity. In addition, the rush toward market-sector provisions fueled by capital looking for investment opportunities may have become more sophisticated. Business failures are making investors more suspicious of the "latest thing," but the complementarity of public and business provisions will be recognized and incorporated into planning. Nevertheless, reduced residential space along with oncoming cohorts' diverse schedules and interests will get many people out of their homes and into various activities and programs. The major counter-current is limited time, especially for two-income families and single parents. Much more targeted provisions will have to accommodate the emerging diversity. Further, since childrearing periods will continue to be shortened, adult recreation will be emphasized more.

At-home Recreation

The aging of the population along with more electronic entertainment devices will increase the significance of at-home activities. Recreation in and around the home is available "on demand" rather than according to institutional schedules. Such flexibility as well as ease of access and low cost make residence-based activity central to most leisure styles. Technologies and provisions that enhance at-home opportunities are consistent with current leisure styles and can be fit into timetables without major conflict.

Cohort analysis

Several cohorts merit special attention:

(1) The baby boom cohort will be moving through the Establishment period in the next 15 years. By the year 2000, the leading edge will be in that Pre-retirement period with time and financial resources at a peak. The unique size of this cohort will result in surges of participation in their favored activities while they are in their 30s, 40s, and 50s. The impacts of parenting will be followed by the relative freedom of the post-parental period. Since most will tend to have only one or two children, they will likely be a major market for developmental activities and experiences for the children on whom they will tend to devote so much attention. At the same time, most women in this cohort will remain employed during childrearing, divorce rates will remain substantial, and single parents will seek recreation in greater numbers.

(2) The current post-parental and pre-retirement cohort is recognized as a special market segment. They are more involved in leisure and more prepared to invest time and money in their recreation than any previous cohort in their 50s and 60s. They will

likely remain relatively active as they enter retirement and will be "active oldsters" in greater numbers than any previous cohort. At the same time, they will have greater financial resources than their predecessors and will be attracted to travel-based recreation opportunities. The caveat, however, is that they are also the first cohort whose white-collar and blue-collar workers will experience forced early retirements. As a consequence, some may have more time than income.

(3) The current "entry" cohort seems to be experiencing particular difficulties in surmounting the thresholds of viable employment, perhaps because so many jobs are filled by the big boomer cohort in an economy that is not growing. Unless that trend is reversed and opportunities enhanced for this cohort, they may develop their own set of characteristics in response to the combination of high expectations and limited opportunities. The impacts on leisure styles are certainly not known at this time, but they will come.

Market segments

The activity-by-activity target market analyses in the previous chapters show considerable consistency:

1. The poor and the frail are not viable markets for many recreation programs or provisions.

2. The High End segments are usually well-supplied. They have learned to use their affluence to purchase access to the best environments and the most attractive opportunities. They can pay to travel and use private facilities to avoid crowding. Although they are important for marketing many kinds of recreation resources, their markets tend to be relatively well-established.

3. The markets with the highest potential, therefore, are found among the Discretionaries. Many are "New Class" in the sense that they are the first generation in their families with college degrees and special skills that are at a premium in the labor markets. They have developed wider interests and new talents in their educational histories. But those in the earlier phases of their careers, however, cannot afford the same recreation costs as the wealthy. They will spend time and money on leisure, but will

remain price-conscious. On the other hand, they will travel, adjust their schedules, leave their children (temporarily), acquire new skills, and explore different experiences. They are the prime growth market for many kinds of recreation opportunities.

4. The Middle mass, however, should not be ignored. They invest in their leisure, but their interests may be more prosaic. They are somewhat more likely to be family-centered. Nevertheless, they do take vacations, plan weekends, and acquire equipment for their activities. In fact, for some traditional activities such as hunting, they are the major residual market. As entrepreneurs cluster around the presumed recreational needs of the affluent, the Middle mass may constitute the least saturated markets for many kinds of public and market-sector offerings.

Stylistic Continuities

Again, continuities may not be as exciting as changes, but they are a lot more common. For example, females are moving more into team sports, although males still produce far and away more demand for facilities and programs. Camping styles are becoming more diverse, but parents with children are still a major market segment. More people are flying to special recreation environments, but 80 to 90 percent of vacation trips are still by car.

Stylistic continuities are based on culture, education, social position, place in the family life cycle, opportunities, and a number of other factors. Some of the most significant continuities are:

1. Teens will continue to explore their sexual identities and seek cohort identification in music and other media products.

2. Young adults seek intimacy, with or without marriage, in a variety of settings that bring them into contact with "their own kind."

3. Parents transform their schedule and resource allocations to engage in activities of sharing and nurture with children.

4. Post-parental adults seeking to employ their freer resources for investments of meaning in what is now recognized as the limited time remaining in the life course.

5. Retired men and women must replace the associations and timetables of the workplace.

6. The frail elderly become more and more constricted in the geographical and social range of their lives.

These central continuities should not be forgotten as we give attention to changes and differences.

Stylistic Changes

Many changes are based on the higher education levels of each succeeding cohort. More diverse interests characterize each cohort, especially those with some experience in four-year colleges and universities. Among the stylistic changes that will affect recreation in the remainder of the century are:

1. Greater attention to self-development. This includes physical and health development as well as learning and the arts. No "revolutions" — fitness or otherwise — have turned time and money allocations upside down for any cohort across the Discretionary and Middle mass range, but trends exist toward attention to the self and to investments in the development of dimensions of the self. Health is a significant dimension of this change that developed first among Discretionaries in their 20s and 30s and spread across the adult population.

2. More diverse leisure styles. The "core" remains with accessible activity that occupies most discretionary time for adults. The "balance," on the other hand, is becoming more diverse: it's now acceptable to do things differently from others in one's household and social groups, at least among most of those with college educations. The range of choices considered acceptable is widening on most social status levels.

3. Greater activity in the later life course. Those in their 50s are less likely to accept definitions of being "old" and limited. Retirement-age adults look forward to more open times in which they may travel or engage in physically and mentally active behaviors. It is a mistake to assume that participation rates of those entering their 50s and 60s during the 1990s will be the same as they were in the 1970s or even the early 1980s.

Resource Changes

Two contextual dimensions of recreation are somewhat problematic: the political and the economic.

1. Political decisions may have considerable impact on many kinds of recreation. The federal government manages great expanses of land and water. Policies for management including opening and closing access, investment in recreation amenities, attempts to recover costs through user fees, and responses to particular recreation groups that seek special opportunities or resources are all part of the political process. On the community level, user fees, investment practices, special interest groups, and planning to preserve and use resources all affect recreation opportunities. The current trend is toward more reliance on user fees to recover costs and on reduced direct expenditures on recreation. Continuing that trend for another decade will reduce opportunities for some kinds of activities and for some lower-income participants. Political policies, then, can and will impact future recreation participation.

2. As noted, economic conditions also have significant impacts on recreation participation. The distribution of income and wealth determines markets for cost-intensive activities. The general state of the economy is the context for the production of investment capital as well as aggregate consumer spending power. A serious recession that lasts five years or more would change almost every projection in this book. No set of resources — public or market, household or individual — is unaffected by the state of the economy. Certainly, neither the national nor the world economy can anticipate unlimited growth in the remainder of this century. Economic limits, continued disparities in resources, and cycles of economic activity will shape and reshape the income patterns of every household.

LIMITATIONS ON THE PROJECTION PROCESS

All sorts of limitations have already been outline. Data sources are incomplete and often inconsistent. Trends are not linear and subject to change. New factors will appear, such as technologies and promotion efforts that cannot now be predicted.

As a consequence, projections might well be classed as relatively likely, probable, and "off-the-wall."

For the most part, our projections are quite conservative. Well-established trends in participation are assumed to continue unless identified limiting or expansion factors intervene. The well-documented "activity/product life cycle" model can estimate the future for those activities that have demonstrated considerable recent change in participation rates.

There are, however, ways in which demand can be created. The first is by a new technology. Home videos have created new markets with a technology that is thoroughly consistent with current lifestyles. Applications of a new material such as fiberglass have dramatically lowered the time and financial costs of boating. At the same time, many new products fail to gain markets. It is almost impossible, then, to predict the impacts of technologies still on the drawing board.

Demand can also be created by marketing. Planned promotion combined with media attention created markets in the field of exercise programs and equipment. Activity and accompanying symbols such as shoes and "designer sweats" became attached to a valued lifestyle. The symbols were not only marketed directly, they were indirectly promoted to market other products. Marketing responded to demand and helped create it. Again, it is difficult to predict just which activities may be the fortunate recipients of such media attention and multi-source promotion.

Perhaps even more important, all the data and analyses in this book reflect the national level. For planning and investment in a particular time and place, this is only background. An analysis of the composition of the population of a given area, current leisure styles and investments, competing and complementary resources and opportunities, and local trends requires study of that time and place. This can often be reasonable in time and cost, and there is no substitute for assessing the particularities of a market area.

Perhaps one last limitation may be in order, simply reinforcing the message of Chapter 2: recreation choices and resource allocations are always in the context of demographic, economic, and social continuities and changes. Projections of recreation that are taken out of these contexts have small chance of success. On the other hand, recreation has its own integrity. Projections should not neglect the current research base in leisure: psychological, sociological, and economic. Recreation is too complex a set of behaviors for any simplistic analysis.